Twayne's United States Authors Series

Sylvia E. Bowman, *Editor*

INDIANA UNIVERSITY

Elder Olson

ELDER OLSON

By THOMAS E. LUCAS

Seton Hall University

 **188**

Twayne Publishers, Inc. :: New York

For my wife, Lise, and my son, Thomas, Jr.

Preface

Elder Olson is a man of many talents and many interests. As a young man he studied music abroad with the idea of becoming a concert pianist. At the same time he was composing the poems that a few years later made up his first volume of verse. The unanimously favorable response to that volume, *Thing of Sorrow*, decided him in favor of what has become a career as a poet, critic, and teacher. I first knew Elder Olson as a teacher; and, after twenty-two years, I still have vivid memories of a classroom technique that was in the best Platonic manner. We were often surprised to find, under Mr. Olson's skillfull questioning, that we knew many things of which we hadn't been aware.

Interesting and vital as Elder Olson is as a person, I have had to be content because of space to treat him in terms of his published work as poet and critic. In both cases he has contributed significantly to American and English letters. The loss of biographical material does not present a serious obstacle to the discussion of his work since it has no direct bearing on his critical writings; and, as far as poetry is concerned, Olson has often made clear that he considers biography irrelevant to reading a poet. A typical comment of his from the Preface to a collection of American poems reads:

> The lyric voices the poet's innermost feelings? Precisely how do we know that? This is a historical proposition which in many thousands of instances—such as those of anonymous poems—we cannot possibly verify; what is more, it is frequently controverted in cases where we do know the feelings of the poet. We can and do enjoy lyrics, moreover, without knowing anything about the poet.

In treating Elder Olson as critic and poet, I have taken a frankly positive point of view that concentrates on his contributions; and I discuss his weaknesses only where I thought such discussion would act as a corrective and result in strengthening his position. Elder Olson's criticism is of two sorts, theoretical and practical. After two opening chapters concerned with background materials, two chapters deal with general theories of art and a theory of the drama. These chapters are followed by three more devoted to practical criticism—one devoted to the drama, another to the shorter forms, and a third to the poetry of Dylan Thomas. Of the three concluding chapters, one deals with Olson's early career as a poet, a second discusses his middle and later poems and plays, and a last chapter gives a brief assessment of the high place he should, and will, occupy in the history of American literature.

The parts of the book are related to one another because the background chapters provide materials for understanding Olson's theoretical position; and his theories determine the direction of both his criticism and the content and technique of his poems.

THOMAS E. LUCAS

Seton Hall University,
South Orange, N. J.

Acknowledgments

I would like to acknowledge with sincere thanks Elder Olson's permission to quote from his many published writings. My thanks, likewise, to the University of Chicago Press for permission to quote from *Critics and Criticism, The Poetry of Dylan Thomas, Plays and Poems, 1948-58, Aristotle's Poetics and English Literature,* "Rhetoric and the Appreciation of Pope," "Recent Literary Criticism," "A Symbolic Reading of the *Ancient Mariner,*" "William Empson, Contemporary Criticism, and Poetic Diction," and "*Hamlet* and the Hermeneutics of Drama"; to Wayne State University Press for permission to quote from *Tragedy and the Theory of Drama;* to the editors of *Chicago Review* for permission to quote from Olson's essays on Louise Bogan, Leonie Adams, and Marianne Moore; to the editors of *University Review* for permission to quote from Olson's essay on William Butler Yeats, " 'Sailing to Byzantium,' Prologomena to a Poetics of the Lyric"; and to the National Council of Teachers of English and the editors of *College English* for permission to quote from Olson's essay on Wallace Stevens

Contents

Chronology

1909   Elder James Olson born March 9 in Chicago, Illinois.

1928   First poems published in *Poetry, A Magazine of Verse.*

1934   BA, University of Chicago. First collected poems, *A Thing of Sorrow,* published.

1935   MA, University of Chicago. Friends of Literature Award for *A Thing of Sorrow.* Appointed Instructor in English at Armour Institute of Technology, Chicago, Illinois.

1937   Married Ann Elisabeth Jones (divorced 1948). Children: Ann and Elder.

1938   PhD, University of Chicago. Dissertation: *General Prosody, Rhythmic, Metric, Harmonic.*

1940   *The Cock of Heaven* published.

1942   Appointed Assistant Professor of English, University of Chicago.

1947   Visiting Professor, Heidelberg University, Germany.

1948   Married Geraldine Louise Hays. Children: Olivia and Shelley.

1952   Visiting Professor, University of Puerto Rico. Co-author of *Critics and Criticism.*

1953   Eunice Tietjens Award for Poetry. Professor of English, Chicago.

1954   *The Scarecrow Christ* published. *The Poetry of Dylan Thomas* published. Poetry Society Award for *The Poetry of Dylan Thomas.*

1957   Joint award of the Academy of American Poets and Columbia Broadcasting System for *The Carnival of Animals.*

1958   Visiting Professor of Literary Criticism at Indiana University. *Plays and Poems 1948-58* published. Delivered lectures on tragedy at Wayne State University.

1961   *Tragedy and the Theory of Drama* published.

1963 Editor, *American Lyric Poems*. *Collected Poems* published.

1965 Editor, *Aristotle's Poetics and English Literature*.

1966 Visiting Professor of English, University of the Philippines.

1968 *The Theory of Comedy* published

CHAPTER 1

Backgrounds

I *The Chicago Critics*

The critical movement in which Elder Olson was and is a shaping force began at the University of Chicago in the middle 1930s. The movement originated with Ronald S. Crane who, until his death in the spring of 1967, remained its elder statesman. Professor Crane's last, and perhaps most important, contribution is the two-volume collection of his writings, *The Idea of the Humanities and Other Essays,* published at Chicago shortly before his death. Other leading members of the Chicago group, in addition to Crane and Olson, are W. R. Keast, Richard McKeon, Norman Maclean, and Bernard Weinberg.

The earliest monument of Chicago Criticism is Professor Crane's article, "History versus Criticism in the University Study of Literature," from the *English Journal* for 1935.[1] Professor Crane argues that literary history is by nature concerned with interpreting "past changes in literary conventions and styles." It was Crane's contention that literary history has served the important function of establishing texts and calling attention to overlooked areas of literary excellence, and that "It should not be forgotten . . . that in the recent past, at a time when the reigning criticism both within the universities and without was impressionism of the most irresponsible variety, the growing vogue of historical studies was an important influence in cultivating respect for first hand knowledge and in providing a much-needed antidote to sentimentality."[2]

To Professor Crane, the limitation of literary history, and the reason it is no substitute for criticism lies in its inability to deal with such universals as epic, tragedy, or lyric. Because the province of literary history is, literally, "the way it was," history must be concerned with the changing aspects of things, with *accidentals*. Art products, on the other hand, however differently they may be defined or particularized at different times, are essentially unchanging and can be considered systematically.

Some of the concerns of the Chicago Critics in the middle 1930s might be stated in the following questions: Is it enough for a university student to be made aware of the facts of literature, its names, titles, movements, texts, and dates? Or should his studies, in addition, give him an understanding of the principles of various kinds of writing so that he can distinguish between philosophical, historical, and imaginative works and know what kinds of questions to ask about each? More concretely, is it enough for him to know who John Milton, David Hume, and Edward Gibbon were? Or is it more important to know why Milton made the form of *Lycidas* what it is and what a reader aware of that form should understand and feel about it? Or to understand the structure of Hume's argument in *An Enquiry Concerning the Principles of Morals*, and, perhaps, be able to defend the ordering of its chapters? Or to understand the strengths and weaknesses in Gibbon's treatment of early Christianity?

During my years, 1946-1950, at the University of Chicago, these questions were answered by means of a primarily theoretical, analytical, and intensive approach to literature, philosophy, and history. The activity at Chicago gave the inpression that a critical renaissance was beginning. There was a concerted effort to reexamine the whole structure of the humanities; to understand their relationship to the sciences; and to understand how they might best be made in R. S. Crane's words, "to exert their power of nourishing our minds, refining our sensibilities, and civilizing our actions."[3]

In the area of literary criticism there was an examination of the critical documents in the light of principles, methods, powers, and limitations. The most comprehensive investigation —and the one in which Elder Olson was most active—was of the possibilities of the philosophic method of Aristotle to deal with the problems of literary criticism. This investigation which involved a study of the whole body of Aristotle's writing, was based on the realization that criticism is a philosophic discipline and that, either explicitly as with Aristotle, or implicitly, as with many modern critics, criticism is always part of a larger system of thought which has individual metaphysical, epistemological, and methodological qualities. This first hand knowledge, not only of Aristotle, but of the whole history of philosophic systems, gives the Chicago critics a professionalism which makes many famous modern critics appear, at best, to be talented amateurs, and, at worst, stumblers in critical blind alleys who quite often falsify and diminish the works they discuss. This professionalism is not easy to attain and has limited the numbers of those who have adopted the Chicago method. There is, after all, no easy way to achieve the complex; all the good things, among them knowledge of the arts, require an apprenticeship of labor; and few are willing to make the effort.

II *Critical Pluralism*

The formal statement of the Chicago Critics on the nature of literary criticism, and the rationale for their pluralistic approach, is Richard McKeon's essay, "The Philosophic Bases of Art and Criticism."[4] McKeon examines all the major critical positions and identifies the kinds of problems each is best suited to deal with. Elder Olson writes of this work:

> It was McKeon whose researches into critical and philosophic methodology both established the basis and determined the direction of critical pluralism . . . this was more than a triumph of philosophic exegetics, it was a Copernican revolution in philosophy itself, for its radical investigation of the very bases of critical and philosophic method set the principles, methods, and conclusions of the different systems in clear relation, and made unnecessary, for those who grasped its implications, the adoption of dogmatic, skeptical, or eclectic positions.[5]

The concept just quoted is especially important. Pluralism is a philosophic position, not limited to criticism alone, which posits that all *valid* philosophic positions are mutually translatable.

One of the most commonly misunderstood aspects of Elder Olson's views and those of his fellow Chicagoans is that he and they are pluralists in philosophy and, consequently, criticism; that each of them is commited to the idea that there is a plurality of valid critical positions. The source of the misapprehension is twofold. First, a good deal of work was done in examining and rejecting various modern critics; and, second, the major critical effort to date has been devoted to the possible applications of Aristotle's thought, especially his method for dealing with imitative poetry. A proper understanding of Elder Olson's position requires recognition that neither of these concerns is exclusive in intention or in effect; that to reject a particular critic is not to deny *completely* the validity of his position, nor, conversely, that to exhibit the powers of one method is not to say it is the only method. It should also be remembered that, as intellectual movements go, Chicago Criticism is young. While its predominantly Aristotelian orientation may not change, in the years (or, hopefully, centuries) ahead a fuller exploration by such critics of other methods may occur. Emergent poetic forms may require new methods, or examinations of the propagandistic, social, and ethical effects of poetry may be made, not only by Aristotle's method, but within a number of other philosophic systems.

As I have already argued, the concepts which underlie critical pluralism derive their validity from the fact that criticism is a philosophic discipline.[6] Olson points out that the critical views of Plato, Aristotle, Emanuel Kant, Thomas Hobbes, and David Hume, among others, are not random views but are produced by the *universes of discourse*[7] in which their philosophies are contained. He also makes the point that, while a critical theory may not be directly referable to a comprehensive philosophy, any criticism necessarily involves metaphysical, epistemological, and linguistic assumptions which can be referred and formulated. Because criticism is always the product of a system of thought, Olson proposes that the number of possible critical positions is relative to the number of possible philosophic positions. He then says that this number is determined (1) by the number of aspects (subject matters) of a given subject which can be discussed; (2) by the causal orientation, and (3) by the kinds of argument (dialectic) which can be applied.

To explain, Olson next distinguishes between art as a *subject* and its various *subject matters*. The *subject* in any investigation is the general basis of the investigation, and the *subject matters* are those aspects of the *subject* which actually are investigated. The history of criticism shows clearly that there are a multitude of *subject matters* derived from the *subject*, Art. I will draw briefly on Olson to make the point:

> These remarks may be illustrated by considering the different senses in which the term *poem* appears in discussions of poetry. The primary sense is that of the product of the art, a certain form imposed upon words, whatever the critic takes that to be. But, other critics argue, the product is only one aspect, and perhaps a relatively unimportant aspect, of the poetic art; the issue of real importance is the human instrumentality which produces; and some argue that this is an actualization of potentialities, others that it is the potentialities themselves. The former sees the poet as either active or passive or both; for instance, the poet appears either as a craftman activity making something, or as the mere instrument of his inspiration, or as a combination of the two. For these the true poem is the poetic behavior of the poet. The latter class see the poet simply as possessed of certain faculties or qualities, or as possessed of them in a certain degree, and tend to identify the poem with the mere possession of these.[8]

Regardless of the *subject matter* the critic chooses, he must attempt a reasoned approach to it. Even if two critics choose to discuss the same *subject matter*, it is still possible for them to differ depending on their *causal* orientations. By *cause*, Olson intends one or more or all of the four causes of Aristotle: formal, material, efficient, and final. He says that critics who are concerned with the art product "have thought to explain the product by reference to its matter or medium, to

the subject represented or depicted, its contents, to the depictive method of the artist or some other productive cause, or to
the end or effect of the product; and some have employed
merely one of these causes or reasons while others have
used several or all."[9] The number of criticisms possible in
any case is proportionate to the number of possible combinations of the four causes.

The third limitation on any system of criticism is the dialectic it employs. Olson recognizes only two basic systems of
argument or dialectic. All dialectics, he argues, are essentially
concerned either with likeness or difference in addition to one
type which combines an interest in likeness and difference.
There are "integral" and "differential" dialectics or combinations of them. In criticism, integral dialectics discuss poetry
by referring it to something which has analogous characteristics, but differential criticisms seek to separate it from all
other kinds of writing and to find characteristics peculiar to
itself.

In terms of these three qualities—subject matter, causal
orientation, and type of dialectic—Olson, disregarding the possibilities of almost endless subject matters and combinations
of causes, proposes ten main types of criticism. Four of these
would consider any subject matter under one of the four
causes integrally. Four more would do the same thing differentially. One would consider its subject matter integrally
under all four causes, and the last would employ all four
causes differentially. Olson illustrates from "art-product" criticisms which discuss either the subject or content (formal
cause) of the art product, its medium (material cause), the
artist (efficient cause), or the end (final cause) either integrally or differentially.

Those critics who treat the subject (content) of the art
product integrally find that poetry has principles which it
shares with other things: "Thus Plotinus finds the beautiful
in art [its subject] to consist in the imitation of the beautiful;
but inquiry into that characteristic shows it to be common
also to natural objects and actions, and so upward to the
beauty which is almost indifferentiable from the good. The
ultimate solution of artistic as of all problems thus lies for

Plotinus in contemplation of God."[10] Hobbes, on the other hand, treats the contents or subjects of poems differentially: "Hobbes . . . proceeds by differentiating 'the Three Regions of mankind, Court, City and Country' to differentiate 'three sorts of Poesy, Heroique, Scommatique, and Pastorall.' "[11]

Content or "subject" criticisms determine the solution of all artistic problems by reference to the subject. A single example, the problem of the nature of the artist, suffices: "If the subject . . . in the raw . . . is all sufficient, the only requisite characteristic of the artist is sharpness of observation . . . If it is thought to require order and selection, faculties which permit this (e.g., the imagination) are added; if the subject of art becomes purely imaginary, in the sense of being quite independent of the real, observation drops out; and so on."[12] Furthermore, such criticisms derive the criteria of art from correspondences of its subject or content with one or more of the remaining causes—the medium, the author, or the effect. Olson illustrates by citing those theories of artistic realism which seek an exact correspondence between the effects of art and of reality. "The subject . . . in such systems," he says, "being nothing other than reality itself, art is copyistic, and the work of art is a 'slice of life.' "[13]

In criticisms which are centered on language, which is the medium of poetry, a similar reduction of problems is possible, again either integrally or differentially. Integral criticism of this kind find general criteria for literature of all kinds—poetic, historical, philosophic—on the grounds that all employ language. On the other hand, such critics as I. A. Richards and Cleanth Brooks seek to differentiate the diction of poetry from that of all other forms of discourse, the former on the grounds of its "ambiguity," and the latter because it is "essentially paradoxical."

Those criticisms which turn on the artist—the productive cause—tend to lose sight of the art object which may even come to be thought of as a sort of by-product of the artistic nature. Carlyle thinks anyone who possesses the poetic character is a poet whether or not he writes poems, which is only one way of manifesting the poetic character and not necessarily the chief one. In some of these arguments, Olson continues, the artistic character depends upon inherent qualities: William Hazlitt thinks poetry a matter of genius; Paul Valéry, inspiration. Opposed to such views is that of Sir Joshua Reynolds who sees the artistic character in terms of acquired traits and who tells the artist how to go about developing the skills he needs. Saint-Beuve and Kenneth Burke afford examples of critics who treat the poet, the productive cause, integrally and differentially. Sainte-Beuve considers all aspects of a poet's life in order to explain his whole work, and the upshot is that poetic art is reduced to behavior. Sainte-Beuve, because he operates within an integral dialectic, can ask "What is a classic?" without distinguishing between philosophic, scientific, or other types of works. Burke, whose position that poetry is "symbolic action," is essentially the same as Sainte-Beuve's, employs a differential dialectic and distinguishes the various types of discourse. When the ends of the poetic art are at issue, integral and differential criticisms are again possible. Integral criticisms discover analogous ends in other things men do, or in natural or divine purposiveness; but differential criticisms find the ends of the art (the poetic pleasure which Aristotle describes) to be distinctive.

The eight kinds of criticism discussed so far are all partial criticisms because they attempt to discuss the art product in terms of a single aspect of it: one of the causes of its production. On the other hand, there are comprehensive systems such as the primarily integral approach of Plato and the essentially differential one of Aristotle which permit a full account both of all aspects of art and all its causes.[14]

In a pluralistic sense, the point to be made is that all systems, both partial and comprehensive, are potentially (depending on the skill of those who employ them) valid and useful. The history of criticism shows, says Olson, that, once differences in assumptions and methods are recognized, certain of the partial systems supplement one another. Taken as a whole, the history of criticism provides considerable valid poetic knowledge which anyone working in contemporary criticism ignores at his peril.

In spite of the fact that Olson, from the 1949 "Outline of Poetic Theory" to the 1966 essay just quoted, has been at considerable pains to make his pluralistic views known, the charge is still often made that he and the other Chicagoans are exclusively Aristotelian. Olson is his own best commentator on this charge:

> The Chicago Critics are not "Aristotelians" although they would certainly defend the Aristotelian approach; and they do not see the solution of critical problems in the fusion or syncretism of Aristotelian with any other method of criticism. On the contrary, they posit a plurality of valid critical—as well as philosophic—methods, and seek to differentiate as sharply as possible not merely these but also even the diverse methods which Aristotle himself utilizes in the different sciences . . . More broadly, they would recognize that, still within the system of Aristotle, problems other than poetic—for instance, moral, political, rhetorical—might be posed and solved. But they would insist, also, that a single critical or philosophical system could not exhaust all conceivable questions about art or existence, and that consequently certain questions are best pursued by methods other than the Aristotelian. The pluralism of these critics has often been questioned on the ground that they have disapproved of the critical method of Empson or Brooks; but a commitment to pluralism, . . . by no means entails the necessary approving of *every* system. Nor does it entail, as some have thought, the necessity of actively working in every such system, although as a matter of fact members of the Aristotelian group have produced studies in Platonic, Longinian, Humeian, and other methods.[15]

III *The State of Modern Criticism*

As Olson has said, a commitment to critical pluralism does not commit the critics to any and every method regardless of its worth, nor does it excuse overlooking weakness in critics and criticism where they exist. Several of the Chicago Critics have worked hard at examining modern critics and have come to definite conclusions concerning their work. One of the earliest of these examinations was the 1939 essay by R. S.

Crane, "I. A. Richards on the Art of Interpretation,"[16] and in 1948 "The Critical Monism of Cleanth Brooks."[17] In the same mode is W. R. Keast's "The 'New Criticism' and *King Lear*."[18] Finally, there are Elder Olson's "Recent Literary Criticism"[19]; "William Empson, Contemporary Criticism, and Poetic Diction,"[20] and "A Symbolic Reading of the *Ancient Mariner*."[21] The following discussion of modern criticism is drawn chiefly from these last three essays.

Two books of critical essays appeared in 1941 and 1942: *The Intent of the Critic*, edited by the late Donald A. Stauffer, and *The Language of Poetry*, edited by Allan Tate. These two books, in addition to essays from their editors, contain characteristic statements from an impressive list of contemporary critics and poets: Edmund Wilson, Norman Foerster, John Crowe Ransom, W. H. Auden, Phillip Wheelwright, Cleanth Brooks, and Wallace Stevens.[22] After an examination of these books, Olson concludes that the critical statements they contain have much in common, despite their authors' attempts to maximize their differences. He thinks, first of all that all the theories they expound are "partial," and that they employ a "universal" method. The "universal" method sees the "form" of literary works in their medium (words) and their "matter" in a bias or interest of the critic. The "form" of a poem can be stated in some kind of stylistic analysis and its "matter" in what the critic thinks it ought to communicate, intend, express, etc. Whatever true differences these critics exhibit are "in the materials of their definitions, in the grounds of their inferences, in the statements of their problems, and in the sources of their criteria."[23]

One of Olson's major concerns is to show how the critics in *The Intent of the Critic* exemplify the common method. Edmund Wilson thinks that literature must be considered in terms of its historical causes and contemplated in a broad social context, while Auden thinks that criticism must be directed to make individuals knowledgeable of past cultures because knowledge in the many is the only check on authoritarian control in an "open" society, whether it be in politics or esthetics. Both Wilson and Auden find, therefore, a social content (subject) in poetry. Norman Foerster has, according to Olson only one theme: esthetic criticism must be coupled with ethical criticism and the value of poetry consists in its having an ethical content.

Ransom's position is less easy to state because it is very vague. Filled out a bit, it comes to something like this: criticism is "ontological," and Ransom explains that the principal "ontological" question arises "when we ask why we want the logical substance of a poem to be compounded with the local substance, the good lean structure with a great deal of texture that does not function."[24] Ransom, who compares poems to "houses and puddings," says the critic must be concerned with the wallpaper and the stuffing as well as the frame and crust. In his metaphor the "wallpaper" and "stuffing" are "local stubstance." He cites the metaphors in Lady Macbeth's proposal of the murder as an instance where local substance is more important than logical substance.

Ransom finds the content of poems to be " 'anything at all which words may signify: an ethical situation, a passion, a train of thought, a flower or landscape, a thing,' and this substance 'receives its poetic increment'; or, as Mr. Ransom suggests one might more safely put it, 'it receives some subtle and mysterious alteration under poetic treatment.' "[25] This "mysterious alteration" is, of course, provided by "local substance; and Ransom's definition is seen to depend on a dichotomy between poetry and prose. Since the content of both is the same, the only possible distinction is a stylistic one. Indeed, a close look at all these critics shows (1) that, though they diversely define their terms, they are discussing poetry as a specific subject matter, not sufficient in itself to allow esthetic evaluation, and (2) that they all turn to style, an aspect of diction, in order to determine what is "poetic." Olson's chief quarrel with the "content-style" dichotomy is that it is always topical; that, while it can be universally applied, it functions only at the level of accident and is not able to produce a definition of poetry.

The objections Olson has raised to *The Intent of the Critic* apply with unimportant differences to *The Language of Poetry;* and it is, therefore, unnecessary to be detailed about that book. Olson finds it amusing, however, when Allan Tate writes these lines in his preface: "The symposium came to a unanimous decision on one question, but it is the main question: that poetry, although it is not science, is not nonsense."[26]

To this point, Olson's comments on contemporary criticism have been reflective and ironic; but, when he considers Robert Penn Warren and William Empson, a note of exasperation appears in his voice and his sarcasm is undisguised:

> How Warren arrives at his conclusion is obvious; in his simple world poems either have a moral or they are mere toys, and no Puritan was ever so flat and dogmatic about the matter. Deny Warren's contention of a moral, and a trap opens to drop you into the abyss of absurdity. But, I protest, Griggs and Lowes are "refuted," not because of any absurdity in their statements or fallacy in their inferences; they are so only through Warren's introduction of a wholly untenable exclusive disjunction and through his complete distortion of their utterance.[27]

Olson's most direct and clear attack, however, is on William Empson's *Seven Types of Ambiguity*, a book which is still, incredibly, influential. Olson describes the theory underlying Empson's position as a reduction of all poetic considerations to those of poetic diction and as a further reduction of all problems of diction to that of ambiguity in its several forms:

> The method might be described as the permutation and combination of all the various "meanings" of the parts of a given discourse . . . The instrument by which he detects the possible meanings of words is the *Oxford English Dictionary;* although it is seldom mentioned by name, its presence everywhere is neither invisible nor subtle. Its lengthy lists of meanings seem to have impressed no one so much as Empson. Apparently he reasons that, since poetry is language highly charged with meaning, the poetic word must stagger under the full weight of its dictionary significances.[28]

The most famous example Olson chooses from Empson's book and the one about which he makes one of his most pungent comments is that in which Empson expounds on the speech in which Macbeth, meditating the King's murder, says: "If tɪɪ Assassination / Could trammel up the Consequence, and catch / With his surcease, Success; that but . . ." Empson comments:

> . . . Words hissed in the passage where servants were passing, which must be swaddled with darkness, loaded as it were in themselves with fearful powers, and not made too naked even to his own mind. *Consequence* means causal result, and the things to follow, though not causally connected and, as in "a person of consequence," the divinity that doth hedge a king. *Trammel* was a technical term used about netting birds, hobbling horses in some particular way, hooking up pots, levering, and running trolleys on rails. *Surcease* means completion, stopping proceedings in the middle of a lawsuit, or the overruling of a judgment; the word reminds you of "surfeit" and "decease," as does assassination of hissing and "assess" and, as in "supersession" through *sedere*, of knocking down the mighty from their seat . . . The meanings cannot all be remembered at once . . . [29]

Olson comments:

> Such a passage as this needs only attentive reading to make manifest its utter absurdity; but then that very absurdity in a fashion protects it, and gains a certain credence for it; it is so absurd that we in a measure believe it, merely because we are loath to believe that anything could be so absurd . . . We are actually being asked to believe that the speech actually *means* all these various things; that Macbeth, trembling on the brink of murder, and restrained only by his fears of what may follow, is babbling of bird-nets, pothooks, levers, trolleys, assessments, lawsuits, and what not; and all this on the shadowy grounds that the OED, or whatever dictionary, lists alternative meanings for 'trammel,' 'surcease,' and 'assassination,' and that poetic language is ambiguous.[30]

Olson concludes that "to deal rigorously with Empson's ideas, to attempt to state them clearly . . . is in a sense to be very unfair with him. It is unfair, perhaps, even to inquire into his exact meaning. As a matter of fact, I am not sure he means anything exactly."[31]

To summarize, the state of contemporary criticism—as Olson sees it—is in much the same condition as was early Greek philosophy when the philosophers, like Thales who thought water the basic substance, reduced the universe to one or two principles and sought to explain everything in their terms. Most modern criticism, employing a style-content dichotomy, tends, either (1) to concentrate on the medium of poetry (words) and, consequently, to explain poetry as a special kind of language, or (2) to the analysis, based on conjectures as to its subject matter, of poetry "as myth, knowledge, as experience or something of the kind."[32] The problem is that, while such partial hypotheses may contain some truth, they are still inadequate. Language, for example, is only the medium of poetry, and to try to find the form of the poem in it alone is like attempting to "infer the shape of the house from the shape and weight of the bricks."[33]

Finally, the same objections which can be brought against language as the essence of poetry apply to the attempt to make content essential. All subject-matter criticisms are based, like the linguistic ones, on a dichotomy between what is poetic and what is not. Both kinds of criticisms are nothing more than separate developments of the basic hypothesis "that all discourse is differentiable in terms of subject matter and style."[34] Olson, committed though he is to critical and philosophic pluralism, rejects critical systems which betray an ignorance of the history of criticism and which are often more like intellectual parlor games than serious attempts to deal with the poetic arts.

CHAPTER 2

Elder Olson and Aristotle

I A Comprehensive System

A basic element in Elder Olson's negative assessment of so many modern critics is their alleged lack of philosophic orientation—a lack which has caused many to mistake the part for whole and to write, at best, fragmentary criticisms, or, at worst, utter nonsense. As a pluralist, Olson does not disapprove of all partial criticisms. He finds great insights and a good deal of merit, for example, in such partial and qualitative critics as Longinus,[1] Plotinus, John Dryden, Sir Joshua Reynolds, Charles Sainte-Beuve, Cardinal Newman, and Matthew Arnold, among others. David Hume, who is a great favorite of Olson's, is something of an exception in that, though he has a comprehensive system of thought, his treatment of poetry is partial, confining itself to effect or final cause.

Nevertheless, it should be made clear that Olson is most comfortable, both theoretically and practically, with all the conveniences that full systems of thought can provide. He is thoroughly at home with Plato,[2] Aristotle, Hume, and Kant, to name no more; and he thinks as a pluralist that these and all validly argued philosophies are mutually translatable. But the best way to demonstrate what Olson has in mind when he speaks of comprehensive systems of thought is to outline Aristotle's general position and also his view of poetry. Such an outline also provides a basis for illustrating the many ways in which Aristotle has influenced Olson as critic and poet, for he is nearly always a presence in Olson's work, either explicitly or implicitly.[3]

A good place to begin the discussion of any philosophic

system is with the question: "What is the nature of knowledge?" Aristotle's answer is that, in the knowledge process, the senses take the impression of the form of an object without taking its matter (as wax can take the impression of a seal without taking the metal); the imagination then takes the image or phantasm which accompanies thought; and, finally, the intellect, as agent, extracts the essence (whatness) of the object. Once the essence is recorded in the intellect, regarded as passive, the object can be returned to and known in its particularities (once Socrates has been recognized as a man, he can be known to be the philosopher, husband of Xantippe, and so on) though never completely, for particulars are accidental, changing, and infinite in possibility. Human knowledge, though of essences is always drawn from the particular and individual, and provides materials on which the sciences are based.

For Aristotle, then, intuition is the first step, the basis for the inductive part of any science. In *scientific* inquiry, principles arrived at inductively are examined deductively (necessary inferences in terms of the four causes are made about a subject) to determine what attributes inhere in a given subject. Aristotle employs a primarily differential dialectic; and, after he has distinguished the nature of scientific knowledge in general, he is faced with the task of distinguishing the various sciences, and the variations in method they involve, from one another.

The result of these distinctions in large terms is the division, based on their subject matter and ends, of sciences into those which deal with *knowing* (metaphysics, mathematics, natural sciences); *acting* (ethics and politics); and *making* (all artificial things, applied and fine arts, between which he does not distinguish). This arrangement is hierarchical in terms of the quality of knowledge involved, as Olson explains and comments:

The theoretical sciences . . . differ as they may in certain respects from each other, are alike in that they involve necessary propositions and have knowledge as their end. In the practical sciences of ethics and politics, knowledge is subordinate to action . . . and in the productive sciences, which are the arts . . . the end is neither knowledge nor action, but the product to be produced. As the practical sciences are less exact than the theoretical, so the productive are less exact than the practical . . . [and] derive many propositions from both theoretical and practical sciences.[4]

It should be kept in mind—and, indeed, this is a great strength of comprehensive systems—that different aspects of a single subject may fall under different sciences. This fact becomes clear in Olson's treatment of the lyric and drama; but briefly, poetry, a single subject, has many aspects: the mode of being of a poem is properly a metaphysical consideration; the explanation of its effect on a human perceiver is a psychological one, and its functions as propaganda, or as a moral force, fall under the sciences of politics and ethics, respectively.

II *Aristotle's* Poetics

With Aristotle's general views outlined, it is possible to talk specifically about his treatment of poetry. However, some general knowledge of Aristotle's method of treating the arts is necessary to understand how that method applies to poetry. This knowledge of method, moreover, is essential to Olson's views; for it is Aristotle's method which interests him most and which he extends to discuss the lyric and the drama as they have developed since Aristotle's time. It is, therefore, necessary to quote quite fully what Olson says on the matter of method:

Now, art, according to Aristotle, is a state concerned with making, involving a true course of reasoning; and it is precisely this reasoning universalized, . . . which is in a sense scientific reasoning of the productive kind; the reasoning part, that is, not the making part; for the latter is not knowledge, and it depends rather upon skill and experience. By "course of reasoning" Aristotle means, naturally, not the psychological processes of the individual artist, for these are incidental to the individual and cannot be formulated, but the course that would be followed in correct, true, and appropriate reasoning about making a given product. Since the arts propose not productions merely but also productions excellent of their kind . . . such reasoning will have to include not merely the "nature" of the thing intended but its excellence as well.

The scope of any productive science, therefore, is the rational part of production centering in, and indeed based upon, the nature of the product; and the structure of such sciences may be described as hypothetical regressive reasoning, taking for its starting-point, or principle, the artistic whole which is to be produced and proceeding through the various parts of the various kinds to be assembled. The reasoning is hypothetical because it is based upon hypotheses: If such and such a work, which is a whole, is to be produced, then such and such parts must be assembled in such and such a way; and if the work is to have excellence as a whole, then the parts must be of such and such a kind and quality. The reasoning is regressive because it works backward from the whole, which is to exist, to the parts which must have existence previous to that of the whole.[5]

When Aristotle's *Poetics* is examined, Olson points out, the procedure just described can be seen clearly: "Chapters i-v are concerned with establishing the definition of tragedy, which is given in chapter vi; chapters vi-xxii resolve tragedy into its proper parts; chapters xxiii-xxiv offer a treatment of epic based upon that of tragedy; and the final chapters conclude with critical problems relative to both forms."[6]

Because Aristotle concerns himself with *imitative* poetry exclusively, some words on the nature of the imitative process, as Aristotle views it, are in order. Aristotle says the arts *imitate* nature in order to remedy her defects. Thus man, ill equipped by nature to move rapidly over the long distances of his world, makes automobiles and aircraft to extend his capacities. Aristotle's view of what the word *imitation* stands for in its application to *all* the arts is, in Olson's words, "that the causes and productive processes of artificial objects resemble those which nature would have evolved had the products been natural and not artificial."[7] In other words, just as nature imposes form on matter in the production of natural things, so does the artist impose form on matter by a similar process, to make artificial things.

But, of course, a poem differs from a pair of shoes as an imitation of nature. Because the poet is concerned not only with imitating a natural process but with imitating an object from nature as nature would have made it had nature to be concerned with the "probable and possible," with what "could or should be," the meaning of the term *imitation*, though still univocal, is extended in the *Poetics*.[8] If the poet is, or can be, concerned with what "could be," several areas are opened to him in which poetic imitations can be made to remedy the defects of nature. It is possible, though neither Olson nor Aristotle has said it directly, for the poet to fashion his imitations of human activities in accordance with an ideal conception: the capacities of his personages for speech, thought, and feeling, for example, can be extended in ways in which they are not found in nature. Is there any natural man, for instance, whose capacity for speech equals that of Hamlet, or whose moral indignation is as intense as that of Captain Ahab? Olson seems to be hinting at this idealizing power of poetic imitations when the speakers in his dialogue on symbolism discuss a bust of Socrates:

> I should rather say it was an imitation, in Aristotle's sense of the term.
> I think I have heard of him and of his sense of the word "imitation." You mean by it, I presume, that the sculptor was not merely concerned with making a likeness of me but wanted also to make a good piece of sculpture, so that the bust, although it does not portray a handsome man, God knows, or portray an ugly man as handsome, is nevertheless a handsome work of art; whereas a copy gives only a replica and is handsome, middling fair, or ugly quite according to the original thing copied.[9]

Once imitation is seen to be the distinguishing characteristic of the kind of poetry that Aristotle is treating, he can begin to build his definition of the species, tragedy. Any imitation must involve three elements: a *means*, the matter of the imitation, an *object*, that which is imitated; and a *manner*, the way in which the object is imitated. Imitative poems use words as means and the actions of men as objects; and they involve one of three manners: narrative, dramatic, or mixed.

Aristotle shows that no one of the three lines of differentiation—object, means, or manner—is sufficient in itself to characterize a species. Certain poems (tragedy and epic) imitate serious actions involving agents who are better than average morally, while certain others (comedy or a poem like Homer's *Margites*) imitate actions involving the ridiculous (mistakes or deformities not involving pain) and agents of less than average moral stature. In terms of objects, then, tragedy and epic are alike; and comedy and tragedy have the same manner. All three ʻemploy verse and, in terms of it alone, are indistinguishable from a writer like Lucretius, Olson's example, who versifies philosophy. It takes all three lines of differentiation to show that tragedy, like epic in objects and means, has a distinctive manner.

These three lines of differentiation are necessary to tragedy. Without them, it would not exist; but of themselves they are not able to define it; its final cause must also be described for it determines form. Aristotle goes on to describe the history of poetic imitations (I have already drawn somewhat from it above) to show how they begin in a natural tendency to imitate and to delight in imitations, through a stage where qualities of objects of imitation are distinguished in moral terms, and, finally, into a stage where artistic form makes for special kinds of final causes or functions.

The final cause assigned to tragedy is that it must arouse "pity and fear" and effect a *catharsis* of these emotions. However, Olson agrees[10] that the fact that tragedies do arouse pity and fear is not an adequate way of describing the full effect of such great works as *Oedipus Rex* or *King Lear*. The tragic poet must also imitate a certain quality of action, involving agents of a certain moral stature, in a particular manner (with its own intrinsic virtues) and in appropriate language. All these requirements, depending on the quality of their performance, add to or detract from the total effect of a particular work. The tragic poet, like all poets, must seek for general excellence. The problem of total effect, depending as it does on a theory of the arousal of the emotions, the quality of seriousness, and general formal excellence, is treated later.

Upon analysis of the "whole" which constitutes tragedy, Aristotle finds it to have six parts, which he takes up in order of their importance. All forms, in his view, have a central or chief part, the quality of which determines the quality of the rest. In tragedy, he finds the chief part to be *plot*, the "soul" of the tragedy, and it determines the quality of all the other parts in that they must be made appropriate to it. The arrangement, then, is subsumptive: *plot*, dominant; *character* (the moral choices of the agents), appropriate to it; *thought*, appropriate to character; and *diction*, appropriate to all the others. *Melody* is related to diction, and *spectacle* (less the poet's than the costumer's art) must be involved properly with the other five. Three of the parts—plot, character, and thought —arise from the object of imitation; two of them, diction and melody, from the means; and the last, spectacle, from the manner.

From these preliminary distinctions, Aristotle then discusses separately each of the six parts of tragedy. In so doing, he introduces criteria of value into the discussion[11] which enable him to treat as better or worse various kinds of plots, characterizations, and so on. Plots can be simple or complex (contain both reversal and discovery). A well-made plot contains both complication and unraveling, and it must depict a unified action (not all actions connected with it, but only those directly relevant); have a definite beginning, middle, and end; and include incidents capable of achieving the catharsis of pity and fear. Thought, which is referred to the *Rhetoric* in some instances and to the *Politics* in others, is considered, in its poetic applications, as within the provinces of those sciences. The diction of poetry is seen as normally distinct from that of either logic or rhetoric.

Before leaving Aristotle, it is proper to treat Olson's interpretation of what Aristotle means by plot, the organizing principle of tragedy, because every imitative poem must have either a plot or something analogous to it and because Olson employs the concept at the heart of his theories of the drama, the lyric, and, in a special way, didactic poetry. Olson thinks that "Aristotle's conception of plot is unique in the history of criticism and that in the innumerable discussions of 'plot' from

his day to our own, his conception is never again attached to
the term *mythos* or any of its synonyms, such as *fabula,
argumentum, argumento, favola,* fable, plot, *Handlung,* and
the like."[12] Considering the history of the concept of plot,
Olson describes some of the meanings it has had which differ
from Aristotle's:

> First, "plot" sometimes has the meaning of the material
> whether historical or legendary, which is given poetic treat-
> ment . . . Again, "plot" often means a tissue of metaphorical
> or exemplary events used as a vehicle for didactic statement
> . . . Again, "plot" has meant the sequence of events simply
> . . this is the sense in which you tell the "plot" of a movie
> . . . Again, "plot" can mean such events as are narrated, or
> as are represented upon the stage . . . Finally, there is "plot"
> in the sense of a string of occasions invented *ficelle*-fashion,
> for the manifestation of character and thought and even the
> use of a special diction.[13]

Aristotle's conception of plot is dependent on the fact that
he is exclusively discussing imitative poetry, and imitative
poetry does not include everything that has or could be
called "poetry" though it does include some things like novels,
the drama, and short stories which many people no longer
consider poetry.

Aristotle, working inductively from the narratives and dramas
of his own day, observed that they were imitative of human
actions. He also noted that these actions were of differing
qualities, some essentially serious, others partaking of the ridiculous. Olson's interpretation of Aristotle's views of the qualities
of actions is better than a paraphrase:

> Now, if actions are serious or ludicrous according to the de-
> gree in which they involve happiness or misery, and if hap-
> piness and misery are functions of the moral characters of
> the persons involved, the imitative action, or plot, cannot
> consist of events simply, or actions simply, but of activity of
> a certain moral quality, such that it produces a particular
> emotional effect; that is, the kind of action includes the kind
> of reasoning and moral principles upon which the choice is

made. *Plot, therefore, in such imitative forms, is a system of morally differentiated activities or actions;* as such, it is indubitably the primary part of such constructions, since it actualizes and completes and gives form to all the other parts, which are related to it as matter to form. (Italics mine.) [14]

Olson concludes his discussion of plot with another reminder that plot is primary (the determinant of form) only in imitative poetry as Aristotle conceives it, and, also, that it can only be understood in the framework of Aristotle's philosophy. All its major terms are dependent on the system of thought and have the meanings which that system assigns to them—serious, ridiculous, happiness, imitative, reasoning, form, choice, to name just a few key terms. In my view, Elder Olson's major contributions both in poetic theory and practical criticism are extensions of Aristotle's thought and new applications of his method.

CHAPTER *3*

Elder Olson's Theories of Art

I *The Proper Bounds of Criticism*

The preceding chapter should make it clear that Olson thinks the critic of poetry can most effectively be concerned with the product of the poetic art, the poem itself. It will be helpful, however, to give Olson's views on the boundaries of criticism: to indicate how he views the roles of the other disciplines concerned with poetry; how he differentiates them from, and yet relates them to, the analysis of poetic form. Olson is most concerned to distinguish interpretation from criticism. Proper interpretation he considers a necessary condition for criticism in that a valid criticism is dependent on an accurate understanding of what a lyric, play, or novel says.

On the other hand, interpretation is likewise subsequent to other disciplines concerned with the establishment of texts and with the problems of their language: "For our purposes there is a point where interpretation begins as well as a point where it ends. We shall assume that it begins where textual and linguistic matters leave off, basing itself upon these, and that it ends where literary criticism proper begins, based upon it in turn."[1]

Much, of course, of what passes for criticism is no more than interpretation that is often of little merit. In the matter of the relationship of interpretation to criticism an analogy can be taken from Zen. The Zen master likens *satori* (enlightenment) to the moon and proceeds to say that, if *satori* is the moon, then what he can say about *satori* is like a finger point-

ing at the moon. It is wise, he concludes, not to confuse the
finger with the moon. Interpretation may "point" to criticism,
but it should not be confused with it.

II *Didactic Poetry*

Olson thinks that there is at least one more major variety
of discourse to which the name poetry has often been applied
which, though it resembles imitative poetry, is essentially different from it. A list of works of this kind would include
Lucretius's *De rerum natura,* a philosophic work; such histories as the chronicles of Wace; ethical treatises like Pope's
Essay on Man; and Dante's doctrinaire *Divina commedia.*
The chief reason these works are confused with mimetic
poetry in modern times is that both kinds employ a similar
diction; and, as many think that poetic quality arises from
the employment of verse, they are all, qualitatively, poems.
The critics who make this kind of judgment feel that values
are involved; that to admit a true distinction between Hamlet
and *De rerum natura* is somehow to denigrate the latter, to
deny its poetic quality. Olson, however, in distinguishing
certain *poems* as didactic as opposed to imitative is not making
a value judgment: "The distinction is not one of value, but
of kind; witness the fact that the *Divina commedia* belongs
to the second class (didactic). The works of the first class
(imitative) are of a quite different order and are constructed
on, and hence have to be judged by, quite different principles
from those of works in the second."[2]
Olson conjectures that, though the two classes of poems
have always been recognizably different, they were first confused when such mimetic poems as Homer's *Odyssey* came
under the scrutiny of early Christian theologians, and literal
readings were found to conflict with Christian doctrine. The
results were allegorical readings and the imposition of Christian orthodoxy (or what that was thought to be), and these
mimetic poems were read as didactic. Olson comments that,
under these circumstances, it is not surprising that all "poetry
came to be thought of as didactic allegory."[3] The extreme of
considering all poetry didactic and the opposite one of fail-

ing to recognize didactic poetry for what it is are forms of the same basic mistake: the search for some universal quality which can make any kind of discourse poetic.

The basic difference between didactic and imitative poems is that the former, "whether allegorical or not, must always either propound a doctrine or determine a moral or emotional attitude toward a doctrine in such a way as to command action in accordance with it."[4] Rather than having a plot as its organizing principle, didactic poetry has a doctrine which it seeks to inculcate either as knowledge or as a spur to action: "Everything in the work mediately or immediately exists and has its peculiar character in order to enforce the doctrine; for instance the argument itself exists only to prove the thesis and is absolutely determined by it."[5]

Olson then states that allegory, far from being the principle of all poetry, comes about when the argument of a didactic poem is presented metaphorically. Such works depend, as do fables and parables, upon extended metaphors: the representation of the process of salvation as an allegorical journey is possible because both salvation and journeys have stages. Some didactic poems may involve metaphorical or symbolic actions which have a superficial resemblance to plot, and they can be read as if a plot were present. However, Olson comments that the action of an allegory, or of any didactic work, is really quite different from a plot. In didactic poetry the characters and incidents must promote the doctrine and be determined by its best interests. Indeed, all the formal elements, which in a mimetic poem are ordered by the needs of its plot—its action, character, thought, and diction—must subserve the controlling doctrine and be appropriate to it.

Another substantial difference between didactic and mimetic poetry lies in the way each involves moral attitudes. Imitative poems depend for their major effects on recognition of the moral quality of their actions and agents. Didactic poems, on the other hand, seek to form moral attitudes with respect to the doctrines they are propounding. The language of didactic allegory, Olson concludes, unlike that of mimetic poetry which is only ambiguous when the necessities of the poem make it so, is always "many-meaninged" because the things to which its language refers always stand for something further. To summarize, didactic poems often superficially resemble imitative poems; but not a plot but an argument based on a doctrine controls the didactic works. Such poems always seek to modify moral attitudes, and are aimed at imparting knowledge or moving the reader to action.

III   *Some Considerations Prior to a Poetics of the Lyric*

The term *unity* was applied by Aristotle to the action of tragedy when he said that such an action had to be single and exclude all irrelevancies. Poems in general, however, have unity in two more ways: by virtue of their continuity and their wholeness. That a poem has continuity and also that it is a "unified whole" which has proper parts in a proper arrangement are clear. The concept "unified whole," not exclusively a poetic concern, is the basis for Aristotle's and Olson's view of form in which the proper arrangement and quality of the parts constitute the power of the poem to achieve specific effects.

The medium of poetry, as has been said, is words. The medium employed by any art imposes necessary restrictions on it and also affords it certain powers. A painter employing line, color, and mass cannot imitate the course of thought, nor can the tones and rhythms of music be used to draw a face. In respect to the nature of media Olson observes that ". . . speech (the medium of poetry) is either action or the sign of action, character and passion . . . Media are not such things as certain pigments or stones but such as line, color, mass, musical tones, rhythms, and words. The object imitated, therefore, must be some form which these can take or which they can imply by signs."[6]

From what is represented by the words of a poem, the audience or reader receives mental images from which opinions are formed. If the audience or reader is convinced (holds the opinion) that danger is imminent, it feels fear; or, if it believes that someone suffers innocently, indignation and pity.

Olson divides emotions into three classes, mental pains (pity), pleasures (joy), and impulses (anger), all of which arise as opinions vary. To Olson, who argues that opinions involve a prior moral judgment, we either approve or disapprove; "in brief, we side with the good against the bad, or in the absence of significant differentiations of moral character, upon grounds still moral, as with the oppressed against the oppressor."

On these psychological and ethical grounds, Olson classifies objects of imitation as either serious or comic; with an area between them. As he explains:

> The serious, i.e., what we take seriously, comprises characters conspicuously better or worse than we are or at any rate such as are like ourselves and such as we can strongly sympathize with, in states of marked pleasure or pain or in fortunes markedly good or bad. The comic, i.e., the ridiculous, comprises characters as involved in embarrassment or discomfiture to whom we are neither friendly nor hostile, of an inferiority not painful to us. We love or hate or sympathize profoundly with the serious characters; we favor or do not favor or condescend to the comic. Serious and comic both divide into two parallel classes: the former into the tragic kind, in which the character is better than we, and the punitive, in which the character is worse; the latter into what may be called "lout-comic," in which the character, though good natured or good, is mad, eccentric, imprudent, or stupid, and the "rogue comic," in which the character is clever but morally deficient. These kinds are illustrated in drama by *Hamlet*, *The Duchess of Malfi*, *She Stoops to Conquer*, and *The Alchemist*; the protagonists in these are, respectively, a man better than we, wicked men (the brothers of the Duchess), a good man with a ridiculous foible, and rogues.[7]

In the area between the serious and the comic lie what Olson calls the "sympathetic" or "antipathetic" forms. The basic element in these is that the morality of the characters does not move us so much as the events themselves. Each of the kinds produces its own emotions: tragedy, pity and fear;

the punitive kinds, moral vindictiveness; the "catastrophe" in comedy "is mere embarrassment or discomfiture, and affects emotions contrary to those produced by catastrophe in the serious forms."[8] The comic, however, is not based on the absence of the "serious" but in its "clear contrary." The comic effect, Olson thinks, is achieved when we recognize that something potentially serious is, after all, the opposite of the serious—the "ridiculous"; and, instead of the *catharsis* of tragedy, we experience a *katastasis,* a relaxation of tension.[9] Of course, true comedy, with its reversal of the serious, depends on the possibility of there being something serious to reverse, as do all theories of the absurd. *Great* comedy and *great* tragedy are alike in the seriousness which always attaches to human excellence; each kind contributes its share to the general potential for "human happiness."

Emotions, then, depend on the state of mind of the audience and on the seriousness of what is presented to it. Olson contends, however, that we do not feel emotions in our experience of art because we believe the events to be real, or because we "willingly suspend our disbelief," but because, as we contemplate what art presents to us so vividly, we are *aware* that it is not real; the awareness that art and other kinds of experience differ is at the basis of the special feelings we entertain in the presence of art.

Nevertheless, the degree of seriousness that a poem depicts —the degree to which human happiness is involved, as Aristotle defines happiness—is the basic determinant of the quality of the poem's effect.

To conclude these extra-poetic topics, Olson's thoughts on pleasure as the end of poetry throw further light on the problems of seriousness and evaluation:

> Pleasure, in general, is a settling of the soul into its natural condition; pleasure in poetry results primarily from the imita-. tion of the object and secondarily from such embellishments as rhythm, ornamental language, and generally any such development of the parts as is naturally pleasing. Where the object of imitation is itself pleasant and vividly depicted, pleasure is direct; when the object is unpleasant, pleasure

results from the catharsis or purgation of the painful emotions
aroused in us, as in tragedy. Pleasure is commensurate, in
other words, with the beauty of the poetic form; and distinctive forms, as they have peculiar beauties, evoke peculiar
pleasures.[10]

To those who object to the idea that pleasure is the final
cause of poetry, Olson replies that there are different pleasures:
those of the senses and those of the mind are obviously different in kind. But Olson is not content simply with saying so;
he explains. And, in so doing, he augments what he has said
on the role of the emotions in art, the nature of seriousness,
and the concept of the "total" effect of a work of art. In
terms (1) of the *quality* of the emotions they evoke, and (2)
of the *quality* of the system of moral values they adopt, Olson
makes a further distinction among the kinds of serious and
comic works. "Serious" works which are based on *ordinary*
moral values—the television Western and the soap opera—
are different in value from works based on a *superior* morality.
A similar distinction can be made among comic works: those
which employ the ridiculous and those which are simply gay
and witty. Works based on ordinary morality are aimed at
entertainment alone; they tend to exaggerate (the basis, in
my view, of sentimentality) and to intensify; they are not concerned with richness nor subtlety of intellectual content:

> The "view of ordinary morality" is a crude and superficial
> one. Character and action are taken at face value. The kinds
> of character are relatively few, they are easily distinguish-
> able as good or bad and of a certain degree of goodness or
> badness, the motives of action are few, simple, and obvious,
> and the moral quality of an action can be seen at once, for
> every act is what it seems to be and springs from exactly
> the motive we should have supposed, unless the author is
> deceiving us so that he may surprise us later. Character is
> almost reduced to circumstance: the murder is more horrify-
> ing if the victim is harmless, defenseless, and innocent; the
> custard pie gets more laughter if it hits the dignified dowager.
> The crudest generalizations about humanity often serve as
> probabilities of character and action. Negroes steal chickens,

shoot craps, and are terrified of ghosts; Jews are rapacious and cunning; soldiers are brave, bullies are cowards, and so on. Intensity of effect is everything; and for the sake of that intensity more enduring effects are foregone.[11]

Olson's point is that there are works—lyrics, epics, novels, plays —which do not forego higher effects. Olson uses as examples Robert Louis Stevenson's *Treasure Island* and Herman Melville's *Moby Dick*. The former he finds technically excellent, but the quality of the pleasure it gives is, he contends, inferior to that of the latter:

Moby Dick depends upon a superior sense of human values; that is upon moral perceptions . . . which require maturity, experience, and a good many other things from the reader. A boy can relish *Treasure Island* as much as, perhaps more than, an adult; I do not think that is true of *Moby Dick*.

There is a difference between having an experience simply and grasping the meaning of experience. T. S. Eliot remarks in one of the *Four Quartets*, "We have had the experience, but missed the meaning." That is exactly the distinction I have in mind. The sensational forms give us the experience; the superior forms give us significant experience; and they are superior in the degree that the significance is a superior one.[12]

The whole matter of the intellectual-moral superiority, the "seriousness," of great works is crucial because all mimetic poems are based in one sense on our ability to react, either crudely or subtly, to moral stimuli. All sane humans react similarly to the "good guy" and the "bad guy"; but not all are equipped, at least by nature, to penetrate the soul of Hamlet and to understand the moral qualities it displays nor the intellectual subtlety of the causes which provoke his dilemma.

IV A Theory of the Lyric

Olson commences his discussion of the lyric by stating again the Aristotelian procedure for defining a poetic species.

Before the definition of a given species can be made and its poetics constructed, that species must already be in existence as an object in the same way that tragedy was available to Aristotle. Olson, therefore, reviews the history of the imitative arts briefly, as Aristotle did to lead to tragedy, in order to arrive at a species of lyric poem.

However, some general poetic concepts, as distinct from the extra-poetic concerns just treated, are still prior to consideration of specifics. For instance, Olson points out that Aristotle has dealt only with the "maximal forms" of poetry: tragedy, comedy, and epic, those which imitate a "system of actions." Olson thinks that smaller forms, such as the lyric, can be treated by reducing systems of actions to their constituents:

> Four kinds of action or behavior can thus be distinguished without regard to seriousness or comicality, etc.: (1) a single character acting in a single closed situation. By "closed situation" I mean here one in which the character's activity, however it may have been initiated or however it may be terminated, is *uncomplicated* by any other agency. Most of what we call lyric poetry belongs here: any poem in which the character commits some verbal act (threatening, persuading, beseeching) upon someone existing only as the object of his action (Marvell's "To His Coy Mistress"), or deliberates or muses (Keat's "Ode to a Nightingale"), or is moved by passion (Landor's "Mother, I Cannot Mind My Wheel"). (2) Two or more characters in a single closed situation . . . This parallels the notion of "scene" in French classical drama; here belong all the real colloquies of persons acting upon and reacting to one another (e.g., Browing's "The Bishop Orders His Tomb"), although not the metaphorical colloquies such as dialogues between Body and Soul, etc. (3) A collection of such "scenes" as I have just mentioned about some central incident, to constitute an "episode." (Arnold's *Sohrab and Rustum*) (4) A system of such episodes, constituting the grand plot of tragedy, comedy, and epic which is treated by Aristotle.[13]

All of these actions are complete. The smaller ones should not be thought of merely as fragments of the larger ones, nor should these four classifications, which are differentiations of the object of imitation, be confused with species though they must be taken into account in defining species.

There are three other general considerations upon which the lyric depends: its definition; the depictive (representative) devices available to it; and poetic diction. The lyric has been variously defined, but none of the older critics, from Aristotle to those of the nineteenth century, was much interested in the lyric. Nineteenth-century and even twentieth-century criticisms of the lyric (from John Stuart Mill to T. S. Eliot) say little more than "the lyric is brief, it tends to involve intense emotions, it is the most personal form of literary expression."[14] All these contentions about the lyric are susceptible to qualification or refutation; not all lyrics are very brief ("Adonais"); not all involve intense emotions ("When Icicles Hang by the Wall"); nor are they all autobiographical. In any case, whether the feelings are the "real" feelings of the poet or feigned ones adds little to the understanding of a poem's form or to the enjoyment that results from understanding.

The point Olson makes is that the lyric, like the longer forms, is an imitation of human activity; and what distinguishes it from other forms cannot be such accidental characteristics as he has just dismissed but something arising from its essence—the activity it depicts. In fact, Olson sees the lyric as concerned with the three kinds of activity already mentioned: the verbal, the deliberative, and the passional. These activities are relatively brief; hence, "the peculiar nature of lyric is related not to its verbal brevity, but to the brevity of the human behavior it depicts. Its verbal brevity, in general, is a consequence of the brevity of its action."[15]

Certain other differences follow from this primary one of brevity. The activity of a lyric must not depend on its position in a series of incidents or on an intimate knowledge of the character of its speaker (though the opinion we form of him generally is always a factor in our reaction to a lyric), but must be "immediately intelligible and moving in itself." Olson states that, although lyrics are referred to as narrative or dramatic, and although there is a difference between pseudo-drama and pseudo-narrative and the real things as they are employed in lyric depiction, lyrics are *essentially* narrative and are not intended to be acted out as are true dramas. Because the medium of the lyric is words alone, the visual effects of drama can only be simulated by images; and images have come to be an important depictive technique in modern poetry.

I suspect that, when T. S. Eliot defined poetry as the verbal equivalent of emotion (the "objective correlative"), he meant mainly that a poem may be made up of a train of images selected to evoke the emotion, or complex of emotions, that the poet has decided on in advance. Further, the writer of lyrics cannot expect his readers to react with strong feeling at the same time he expects difficult reasoning from them, nor can he devise too complicated images which are "too elaborate as a whole . . . or composed of too many parts, or of these too intricately related."[16] Olson summarizes by saying: "Novel and drama tend naturally toward the fuller development of invention, a broader scale of depiction, a fuller use of discourse, while lyric tends toward concise invention, economy of depiction, concision of language."[17]

It should be kept in mind that none of the depictive devices used by lyric poets is the exclusive property of the lyric, nor, for that matter, of imitative poetry—all of them can be, and have been, employed by philosophers, historians, and so on. Yet depictive devices, especially as they become part of the *depictive technique* of an individual poet, are extremely important for these reasons: Critical theory—including the treatment of images, metaphors, and symbols which follows—as a branch of philosophy is always conceptual and abstract; but poetry is made up of individual poems which might be described as the particularities from which a reader is prompted to feeling and thought.

When the theory of poetic form which Olson proposes is applied in practical criticism to a given poem, the kind of thing the poet imitates, the "what" of the poem (the plot or its analogues) can only be discussed abstractly apart from the "how," the poet's technique of depiction. Stated another way, in practical criticism, as well as in poetic composition, it seems clear that the critic, as well as the poet, must inevitably think of "what" in terms of "how." The "how" seems virtually inseparable from the "what" in a practical sense. The "how," the representation or depiction, is the particularization of the "what"; and from it the moral quality (emotional and intellectual) must be read. The foregoing is made clear by Olson's practical criticism. He always illustrates the activities that a poem imitates with particular instances of how it does so, and he also devotes a major effort to depictive techniques as a separate subject matter.

An "image," says Olson, "is a verbal expression capable of conveying a conception either of some sensory perception or of some bodily feeling."[18] Sensory impressions include all the senses "as when a sight, sound, taste, and so on are imagined"; "bodily feelings" include "pressure, motion, weight, heat, cold, vertigo, lassitude, energy, or the bodily conditions attending particular emotions."[19] In an Aristotelian sense, which is the way Olson intends it, an image should be like the source of a direct perception from which the intellect can extract the essence. An image differs from a description because its immediate appeal is to the imagination while description appeals, more or less directly, to the intellect. If a writer tells us, for example, that the ice is a hundred feet high, he describes it; if he speaks of the ice as a mast high, he makes an image.

Olson distinguishes images into two classes—those which present a direct and objective perception and those which are modified by the character or state of the poem's speaker. In the second class, an additional differentiation can be made in terms of emphasis. Either, Olson says, "we primarily conceive the object (though modified) to be possessed of certain qualities, or . . . we primarily interpret the perception as significant of the condition of the perceiver."[20]

Within the two classes of images there are many ways in which the structure of an image can be varied:

> All these kinds of images permit various modes of construction, which seem to cause the imagination of the reader to operate in different ways. It may be worth-while to note a few of these: 1) images based on comparison in which we are forced to imagine one thing as a standard for another, as

in 'ice mast high'; 2) those based on mental transit from cause to effect, whenever the cause is in some way remarkably potent for good or evil, or remarkable simply, as in Bogan's "Like fire in a dry thicket / Rising within women's eyes"; 3) those based on transit from effect to cause, under the same conditions, as in Keats' "And the long carpets rose along the gusty floor"; 4) those based on dynamic interrelation, as in "And owls have awakened the crowing cock."[21]

Olson thinks that, for the images of poetry to achieve their greatest effect, they must involve heightening or slight exaggeration. Olson bases his contention about heightening on the Humeian concept that "mental images" are necessarily fainter than real perceptions; hence, they require reinforcement to be moving.[22] He uses Wallace Stevens' "rouged fruits in snow" as an example of an image with the right degree of vividness achieved through the uncommon juxtaposition of the words, concepts, and experiences which it contains. The whole matter of the vividness of poetic imagery, as opposed to the vividness of ordinary perceptions, is an interesting one. Olson agrees, in a qualified way, that the vividness of Stevens' image is of an intensity greater than the sight of an apple in a snow bank would produce, however startling such a sight might be.

As far as metaphor, a second device of depiction, is concerned, Olson follows and extends Aristotle's discussions of the subject in the *Rhetoric* and in the *Poetics*. Olson sees metaphor, generically, as based on likeness either in fact or at least such likeness as is discernible by thought. Consequently, all metaphors involve three elements: "the 'referent,' or thing analogized; the 'analogue,' or thing to which the referent is analogized; the 'continuum,' or ground of likeness . . ."[23] Aristotle designated four basic kinds of metaphor, all based on likeness, the first three of which involve the transference of the name of one thing to that of another, either 1) from genus to species; 2) from species to genus; or 3) from species to species.

Olson doesn't elaborate on these first three, but Aristotle's fourth kind of metaphor, the "analogical" or "proportional" variety, he divides into two sub-kinds, simple and complex. To Olson, "'pearl pale hand' is simple, whereas 'angelic hair' is complex; the former sets only a certain pallor before us, whereas the latter suggests sheen, delicacy, length, color, etc. Complex metaphors give us either a mere conjunction of attributes or a correspondence of whole with whole and part with part."[24] A good example of the latter is the metaphor from Browning's *Mr. Sludge the Medium* in which youth and age are analogized to a waterworks: youth has wellsprings of water; age is a labyrinth of pipes through which water might be played, but, sadly, the wellsprings are diminished.

Olson points out that metaphors can be constructed to delay the disclosure of vital knowledge and, hence, to create suspense in a poem. The poet makes such difficult metaphors, Olson thinks, in three principal ways: either through "omission of one of its elements, through unclear statement grammatically, [or] through apparent falsity."[25] This last usage is well exemplified in the practice of the "metaphysical" poets. As Olson observes, "Anyone knows that the sun is like a lamp in respect of light; but why a flea is like marriage, or why lovers resemble compasses, is another matter. The metaphysical metaphor takes referents and analogues with no apparent continua; or states the continua last."[26]

The final depictive device, symbolism, is especially interesting because the modern tendency is to find symbols everywhere. Olson has definite views as to what constitutes symbolism and as to how it is best used in mimetic and didactic poetry. Where metaphor is based on likeness, symbolism does not involve it but results from the transference of the concept of one thing to something else which it is unlike but to which it can be related in order for the transference to be intelligible. On a very simple level, a flag, certainly not on a basis of likeness, can be said to symbolize a nation; or, on the grounds of being a part or a cause, the keystone can symbolize the arch, and so can the tools or equipment used symbolize a trade or profession; hammers and saws are good symbols of carpentry; and the mortar and pestle of pharmacy. Because, however, the concepts of symbols are basically unlike, the symbol maker must give an indication of his intent, just as a cartoonist who draws a circle must add shading if he wants it to be taken for a sphere.

On a more sophisticated level, the symbol maker must not only have some concept which he wants to symbolize but must determine what emotions he wishes to be evoked by his concept. Even death can be made to arouse contradictory emotions as it is presented as either terrible or beautiful as symbolized by decay and putrefaction or by transcendently splendid things. After the symbolist has studied the concept to be symbolized to determine the way in which he wants it understood and felt, he must find or invent something with which to equate it. In "A Dialogue on Symbolism," Olson has Socrates state the definition of symbol:

> Suppose, for example, that a symbol-maker conceived of a certain way of life, which concept he wished to symbolize; and suppose, on casting about in his mind, he thought it best typified by the kind of life led in a certain city—say, Byzantium. Now, it seems to me that if his thought runs on "life such as that at Byzantium," he has only an example; if on "life like that at Byzantium," only an analogue, so that, putting it into words, a metaphor will result; *but if he so frames his conception of Byzantium that it is not a mere mirror, as examples and analogues are, but, as we see the thing he truly intends; then and then alone has he made a symbol.*
>
> You seem to think that symbols are not, after all, metaphors.
>
> And should I? Whatever name we give to our symbol will now apply immediately to the symbolized, and thus differ from metaphor; for a metaphor is only the name of a certain thing transferred to its similar in respect to a certain similarity, although their concepts remain distinct, whereas the name of the true symbol will not stand metaphorically but directly for the symbolized; because the concept of the symbol has been identified with that of the symbolized.[27]

All of the things said so far of symbolism are applicable to its use in any form of discourse; its direct applications to poetry must, therefore be investigated. As might be anticipated with Olson, the applicability of symbols to poetry depends on the Aristotelian view of imitative poetry and on Olson's view of didactic poetry. The principal part around which a mimetic poem is organized is its plot, or one of its analogues; and the principal part of a didactic poem is the argument which presents its doctrine. If a poet of either variety wishes to make his poem wholly symbolic, he must symbolize the principal part, or he may use symbols at less important levels:

> . . . the characters and their action and, in short, the plot as a whole may be symbolic.
> As in Kafka's *The Castle* or Joyce's *Ulysses.*
> Or there may be symbolism of narrative or dramatic manner.
> Yes; a play called *Our Town* would exemplify that, for, while the plot is not symbolic, the dramatic representation is.
> Or, finally, there is symbolism of diction; for a poet might symbolize brute nature by a tiger or a hawk, and call it by their names; and this could be like metaphor and yet different from it as we have argued.[28]

The distinctions Olson makes between image, metaphor, and symbol are clear and useful ones. Images can be employed in either dramatic or narrative manner and convey something like a direct perception; metaphor, based on likeness, has many uses as a device of depiction; and symbol, which can dominate a poem, identifies one concept with another so that contemplation of the symbol evokes the symbolized. The fact that all three are distinct, however, does not prevent the poet from using them together. For example, a poet can employ images by themselves or combine them with metaphors. Many symbols are treated imagistically; and, though not a metaphor itself, a symbolic structure can contain metaphors. Finally, metaphor can involve the likening of two items depicted imagistically.

In the sense that all three of these devices are constructed from words, they are a part of diction; and, because of their importance, Olson's stand that diction is the least important of the parts of a poem has caused considerable dismay in critical circles. Not only has he insisted on this "heresy," but he has aimed several of his attacks on modern critics at those who find the essence of poetry in poetic diction.

Olson has always been disturbed that his position relative to diction of poetry has not been better understood. He has said on several occasions that, in denying primary importance to diction, he is not denying (1) that unless the reader grasps the meaning of the words of a poem he can never understand its form, and (2) that, though diction must subserve the ends of the poem's other formative elements, an appropriate and excellent diction is essential to a good poem. His care with the diction of his own poems, as he once told me, should be sufficient evidence of the importance he assigns to diction. Nor does he underestimate the need for great use of language if great thought and feeling are to be conveyed.

On the other hand, Olson insists that there is nothing distinctive about the diction of poetry: "There are no devices of language which can be pointed to as distinctively poetic; any other kind of composition may utilize metaphor, images, rhythm, meter, rhyme, or any of the 'devices of poetic language,' and poetry may utilize any of the devices associated with any other literary kind."[29] The only proper way that diction can be said to be poetic is to describe it as it is used in poetry, in its "poetic employment."

In mimetic poems, plot and its analogues determine the effect the poem has; but the emotions produced at a given point in such poem's are dependent also, and perhaps more importantly, on the way in which the plot is disclosed. As Olson asserts, language is one of the devices of disclosure in mimetic poetry. But it is a serious mistake, he argues, to believe that we can gather everything that is being disclosed if we simply grasp the meaning of the words. "Words as meaning" is not adequate as a description of how words function in poetry:

> I have already distinguished . . . between speech as action (*praxis*) and speech as meaningful (*lexis*); to neglect that distinction is, I think, to blind one's self to a great deal of the poetic mechanism. Most of what is termed "meaning" by critics and

poets is not meaning at all, but implications of character, passion, and fortune derived from the interpretation of speech as action. Unless the meaning of words is grasped, we cannot to be sure, grasp the nature of the speech as action, but when we do we make inferences—which, as I have argued, are not *meanings*—as to the character and his situation; we perceive an object which is the principal cause of our emotions in poetry.[30]

Though language has intrinsic qualities in the way of sound and rhythm, to consider diction as speech and speech as action is to consider it most importantly. All accurate interpretations of a poetic text depend on the realization that its speeches are actions and are either *the action* or part of it, and correct interpretation is a prior condition of criticism.[31]

With all this said, Olson turns to the role of diction in poetry simply as diction. Its prime role is that of disclosure: not of how an angry man would talk, but, *given* his anger, how words, as such, can best be used to depict it. Words are a temporal medium; and in a poem, as contrasted with a painting which is spatial, all the parts of its activity are not present at the same time but succeed each other in the reader's attention. Because experiencing a poem is temporal, the whole poem must be remembered if it is to achieve its full effect; its language must be such as not to deny memory. All temporal arts involve anticipation; and it, in turn, gives rise to "suspense and the unexpected," to both of which language contributes. When the theorist, however, is concerned with the employment of language as language alone, he is not concerned with what ought to be disclosed or concealed but only with how language can best function with regard to concealment or disclosure. In summarizing the functions of language in poetry, Olson says the poet can have seven aims in his use of it: "These aims are disclosure, partial disclosure, concealment, direction of attention, evocation of suspense, production of the unexpected, and ornament."[32]

The highest degree of disclosure is achieved when language is employed most clearly, despite the problems of interpretation which may arise when the clear statement is understood. Clarity in language, Olson says, depends on three things: the words, syntax, and the relationships between sentences. Words are clear when they are used primarily and are immediate, commensurate, consonant, and familiar. Olson, illustrates the qualities of "clear" words; words are "prime" when, for example, the noun "dog" is applied to a dog and not to a used car. Words are "immediate" which do not require study before their meanings can be solved. Olson uses Eliot's "poly-philoprogenitive" as an example of a word which must be submitted to etymological analysis to be understood. Words are "commensurate" when they agree in particularity or generality with what they represent. Olson illustrates by saying that the nouns "animal" and "Socrates" are not "commensurate" with "man" because the former is too general and the latter too particular. To be "consonant," words must be used so that nothing other than their literal meanings can be inferred from them. If a pejorative expression is used as praise, it is used unconsonantly and unclearly. "Familiar" words are just that, but they are also familiar words used in the most common ways; a word used commonly as a noun is not so clear when it is used as a verb.

Olson lays down eight conditions for syntactical clarity: that the grammatical construction be familiar; that the order be the common order; that the "material sequence" be observed; that what is predicated and attributed be immediate; that the sentence form be primary; that sentences be complete and unified; that the rhythm stresses should be stressed; and that sentences be of a proper magnitude. Certain of these conditions are self-explanatory, but Olson illustrates those which he thinks are not:

> By observing the material sequence I mean such things as observing the natural order of events; for instance, Shelley's "I die, I faint, I fail" does not observe the material sequence. By immediate predication or attributions I mean that the predicate or modifier lies adjacent to the subject to which it attaches. Thus parenthetical expressions of any length between subject and predicate produce lack of clarity. By unified sentence I mean one which connects matter which ought to be connected. For example, "She mourned his death and subsequently became very proficient in athletics"

is not a unified sentence. By primary sentence form I mean the posing of a question in the interrogative, a statement in the declarative form, and so on. By proper magnitude I mean that the sentence should not be so long that the beginning is forgotten before the end is reached.[33]

The third and last item relevant to verbal clarity concerns the relations of sentences, and Olson lists four ways in which they are related: "additively, qualificatively, antithetically, and inferentially; they either add fresh information, qualify what has been said, oppose each other in some way, or are related as parts of an argument."[34] It is easy to see how the manipulation or violation of the rules for clarity can contribute to concealment or partial concealment and, in turn, to suspense and the unexpected.

After considering general poetics, the next step is to consider the one species of lyric Olson has treated theoretically. To Olson, this species is the "lyric of choice" because he finds the part of such poems which is analogous to the plot in tragedy to be the "moral choices" made in their courses. Olson illustrates this species with Yeat's "Sailing to Byzantium." He says the species is one

which imitates a serious action of the first order mentioned above, *i.e.*, one involving a single character in a closed situation, and the character is not simply in a passion, nor is he acting upon another character, but has performed an act actualizing and instancing his moral character, that is, has made a moral choice. It is dramatic in manner . . . the character speaks in his own person; and the medium is words embellished by rhythm and rhyme. Its effect is something that, in the absence of a comprehensive analysis of the emotions, we can only call a kind of noble joy or exaltation.[35]

In this definition Olson has used all three Aristotelian lines of differentiation; object, manner, and means. The activity of choice is the principal part; and the other parts—character (the moral stature of its speaker), thought (the way he reasons about the choice), and diction (the words and their orna-

ments)—are all made to serve the principal part which sub-
sumes them all. Certain additional requirements of the "lyric
of choice" can be stated; but, it should be understood, that it
is only one of many possible species of lyric which could be
defined in a similar fashion. Some critics have objected that
the idea of poetic species precludes individuality.[36] They are
in error. Each poem is indeed, as I have argued earlier, particular. As a consequence of particularity, individual poems require
individual treatments in practical criticism. The lyric of moral
choice is limited in that it imitates a "serious" activity. The
character of such a poem's speaker, too, must be above the
average, but not so noble as to put him above suffering, for
the happiness of such a one is beyond question.

Olson summarizes: "Moreover, the choice imitated cannot
be any choice, even of a moral order, but one which makes
all the difference between happiness and misery; and since it
is a choice, it must be accomplished with full knowledge and
in accordance with rational principle, or as the man of rational
prudence would determine it.[37] Some of these requirements
of the "lyric of choice" are generic, springing from the nature
of imitative poetry itself, or the general nature of the lyric;
but some of them arise from the needs of this species of
lyric. None of the requirements denies individuality to a
poem; the *efficient cause* of any poem is an individual poet
with an individual mind and technique.

V *The Ethical Function of Imitative Poetry*

Earlier in this chapter, a good deal was said about the total
effect of a poem as distinguished from its particular effect of
evoking emotions for the pleasure of experiencing them or
for their catharsis. The role of and the quality of the pleasure
which results when the form of a beautiful poem is grasped
have also been discussed. What is here proposed is an ethical
function of poetry which depends on its other ends but is
also distinct from them.

Olson's views on this subject have, again, a definite Aristotelian slant, but, this time, with Humeian colorings. To begin
with, man is by nature a social animal who requires the society

of his fellows to survive, especially in infancy. Consequently, every man has a stake in the arrangements (governments) men make in order to live together. For man is not only a social animal but a rational one. Indeed, his ability to reason, Aristotle thinks, distinguishes him from all other creatures. A man, then, if he is to achieve his highest end, must live in accordance with that which is his essence, his reason. His society, therefore, should be of an order to promote his efforts to be a fully developed human being.

The "arrangements" are therefore, reciprocal: the good society requires good men; and men, in order to be good, need the proper kind of government. But, Olson asks, are just laws, religion, and moral political philosophy sufficient in themselves to produce good men? Laws and religion he views as external in that they are in most cases more concerned with the fear of punishment or with the hope of reward than with inner conviction. This assessment may seen cynical, but the point is that there is alway a possibility that the individual who obeys the precepts of civil law or the canons of his church may do so simply from fear or hope, not from true regard for right and wrong. Where such a possibility exists, no apparatus can be *entirely* depended upon to produce the highest attainments for men, for such attainments demand action in accordance with what is good for its own sake.

Up to this point, I agree with Olson's position. However, when he dismisses the power of moral and political philosophy to move men to action because they proceed by reason, he adopts a Humeian stand which I do not think is necessary to his argument nor completely consistent with his view of the "serious" in art. Hume argues that reason can deal only with relations of ideas (Olson has pointed out that Hume confuses ideas with the phantasms that accompany thought) and that the operation of reason in morals is always *ex post facto*. That is, man has a "moral sense" which causes him either to approve or to disapprove of things automatically; and his reasoning has nothing to do with these feelings

Following this line of thought, Olson argues that even though a man has a concept of love or hate neither of these concepts moves him to love or hate; these reactions result

only from the presence of objects by which he is attracted
or repelled. I am not wholly convinced, though I admit that
ideas are "moving" in terms of situations (the particulars
from which they are extracted). It seems to me, however,
that my ability to conceive the ideal of any situation involving
moral choice with reference to such perfections as truth and
justice, and to choose to frame my action in accordance with
that ideal, is more important than my feelings. Plato would
say we have to "recall" these perfections; Aristotle, that we
have to "learn" them and become "habituated" to acting in
accordance with them. I fear I often desire what is not wholly
good, although I will not go so far as to say that I have been
repelled by what reason later would have honored.

As I said, I do not think Olson's rejection of the role of
reason, followed by rejection of moral and political philosophy,
is necessary to his view of the role art plays in producing the
good citizen and, hence, the good society. At this point, Olson
reiterates his theory that our emotions are aroused whenever
we entertain the opinion that such and such, either good or
bad, is the case, and that these opinions are always accom-
panied by visual and mental images: "For example, the sight
or imagination of an animal about to attack will produce fear,
if it is attended by the opinion that it is dangerous and about
to attack one, but without the opinion of imminent danger,
or without the image presented by sense or imagination, no
such emotion will result. Similarly, the image of someone suffering, attended by the opinion that the misfortune is unde-
served, will produce pity; but without these, pity can never
be excited."[38]

Now, I agree with the foregoing, but I think Olson again
underplays the role of the intellect in producing the mental
states (opinions) which produce emotions, and overplays the
role of images; but I again admit that a direct impression, or
a circumstantial account, is more immediately moving than
an abstract concept. As far as images are concerned, and
though visual images are distinguishable from imaginings, some
sort of image accompanies all thought and feeling. And, for
that matter, some feeling accompanies all thought, and all
feeling involves some thought; which one dominates is a matter

of emphasis.[39] I am sure that in such uncomplicated cases as imminent danger, or the sight of suffering, the opinion is formed so rapidly and the emotion is so immediate that the intellectual process is imperceptible, or perhaps, through memory, need not be repeated in each new situation if that situation is similar enough to others which have already been known.

But Olson's lack of emphasis on the intellect in regard to the emotions does not vitiate the major argument which goes forward along more truly Aristotelian lines. A good man, says Olson, is one who "has the ability to see the consequences of good and bad actions, and to distinguish good from bad, and to hold firmly to the course of the good."[40] The man, on the other hand, who acts badly is deficient in these three capacities. A deficiency as to the third of these capacities involves a weakness of the will, which in Aristotle's thought, as Olson correctly states it, "is the absence of a habit of choice." For Aristotle, the habit of right choice is learned behavior, and it is prior to moral activity. A deficiency in the first two, Olson maintains, is "due to weakness of the imagination, and failure to reason out consequences."[41] The images of things which accompany such a person's thought are so weak that he is not much moved by them. As a result, he is either not motivated or is unable to arrive at correct conclusions about them. Such a person is apt to prefer an immediate pleasure, because he fails to see a long term loss in a moral sense. Further, the man who acts badly thinks, usually, that he is acting from self-interest.

Olson sees mimetic poetry as ideal for improving the moral character of persons who act badly, not by teaching by precept as didactic poetry does, but by the vividness with which it presents actions and characters of moral quality. Because poetry forces its audience to side with the good and to reject the bad in a situation where self-interest cannot be involved—the characters in a play, novel, or lyric have no personal hold on a normal reader—it can inculcate the habit of right choice. Because any audience is heterogeneous with regard to moral awareness, general education, and so on, and because, in spite of these differences, they react together in approving the good and in rejecting the bad, and in accepting the probable and rejecting the improbable, the skill of the poet in producing the right climate of opinion with its attendant emotions is essential.

Olson describes the poet's activity as it is related to the ethical function of his art: "Then this art is in its essence true and just; although the dramatist seeks primarily to write a good play, he must necessarily follow virtue in order to do so. And in order to construct a good plot, he must consider the consequences of character and action; all of which he presents in true colors, and as vividly as possible. This, I suppose is the reason why the audience can distinguish so well."[42]

Olson's argument would be stronger had he qualified it to distinguish between poems involving crude and subtle moralities, but his basic approach is sound—moral recognition at any level is a step in the right direction. The poetic art, in its pursuit of the beautiful and the serious, achieves also the end of advancing the good.

VI   *The Humanist*

It is fitting to close this chapter on poetic theories with a brief view of Olson's thoughts on the training and work of the critic, or the "humanist" as he calls him. To Olson, the "humanist" is an adjunct of the artist, and his role is "to interpret and teach what the artist creates."[43] The "humanist" must, first of all, treat his material scientifically in an Aristotelian sense and be able to use "the most exact methods appropriate to it."[44] He must, likewise, be skillful in argument (dialectic), and he must know philosophy, ("the principles, methods, and organization of the sciences,")[45] which necessarily includes a knowledge of metaphysics. Moral and political philosophies are also requisites, and psychology is needed because "art comes from the soul and works upon the soul." The "humanist" must also know all the arts and their histories, but prior to history he must know the theory of forms. Turning to the media of the arts, he must know languages, color theory, and so forth. Finally, he must know the art of his own day for, as Olson says, "Although he will not have the last word on that, he will have the first."[46]

This description of the humanist-critic completed, a question is asked and answered:

> Do you think if he knows all these things, he will be in danger of being disesteemed?
>   On the contrary.
>   Let him earn his honor then, and perform his function. But consider, will he not improve his science, and will that not improve art, and art in turn improve man and Society.[47]

The high and hopeful roles Olson assigns to the artist and to his interpreter-humanist may perhaps seem too optomistic when set against man's dominantly inhumane past and present; but, after all, man's history is infinitesimal; the humanizing effects of philosophy and the arts are unquestionable; and, perhaps, there is time.

CHAPTER *4*

A Theory of the Drama

In making a final distinction between epic and tragedy Aristotle had to rely on the fact that tragedy and epic, alike in other respects, employed differing manners of imitation: epic, narrative; tragedy, dramatic. Olson extends this distinction to indicate the basic difference between poems which are to be acted out and *all* others. He thinks, for instance, that though a lyric can be read aloud, it is primarily narrative and self-contained: it does not depend on acting ability, stage sets, stage directions, and so on.

I *Dramatic Manner*

When a poet has decided to make a play, he takes on all the virtues and limitations of dramatic manner, as Olson makes clear in *Tragedy and the Theory of Drama*:[1]

> The poet, the novelist, and the short-story writer are simultaneously producer, director, actors, scene-designers, orchestra, and even a row of critics, reviewers, psychiatrists, and whatnot commenting upon the show whenever it is useful for them to do so. The dramatist is not. He can outline a general plan of action which directors and actors must make specific in performance, . . . and he can determine what the actors are to say, but not how they are to say it. A poem or a work of fiction is the product of a single art; a drama, when performed, is the product of a complex of arts. (12)

The success of a play is dependent on the success and co-operation of many and various people and arts, and the dramatist can never have more than an imperfect control of all of them. But there are inherent strengths and additional limitations in drama. Olson thinks dramatic representation provides a big gain in vividness; for, he insists, what is directly presented to vision is always more vivid than what can be imagined. To prove his point, he cites Shakespeare's famous description of Cleopatra: "The barge she sat in, like a burnish'd throne, / Burn'd on the water; the poop was beaten gold; / Purple the sails, and so perfumed that / The winds were lovesick with them; the oars were silver, / Which to the tune of flutes kept stroke, and made / The water which they beat to follow faster, / As amorous of their strokes . . ."

Vivid as these images are, and Olson admits that they may be more effective in some respects than direct vision, they are not so clear, vivid, and precise as direct sensation. We cannot tell from them, for example, where the barge is; which way it is facing; the shape of the sails, and so on. The point is, of course, that the dramatist can employ appeals to the imagination along with direct presentation; and it is also true, as Olson observes, that we may *read* of a disaster in which hundreds have been killed without spoiling our breakfast while the sight of a cat killed by a car may ruin our whole day.

This strength of drama, one which results from its direct appeal to the senses, is not invincible. Some things which can be narrated successfully are incredible or present great difficulties when staged. Olson wonders, for instance, how many readers have noticed that, when Billy Bones dies in *Treasure Island*, he falls face downwards and yet, a few pages later, is lying on his back—a flaw that would not go unnoticed in a play. Olson tells, also, of the difficulties which can be caused by such a simple thing as flying a flag on the stage. He cites William Archer: "If it is allowed to hang limp, it mutely declares the stage to be nothing but a stage; if it is set streaming by a fan, it sets the audience wondering about the mechanism which moves it. In either case it takes on an emphasis far beyond its dramatic importance"(18).

Neither of these instances is conclusive, but it is clear that some actions are by nature better suited to narration and others to drama. Olson's next task is, consequently, to define suitably dramatic actions with reference to other characteristics of dramatic manner. First of all, as E. M. Foster points out, actions which are primarily internal are not well suited to the stage. While a novelist may be wholly concerned with what goes on inside a given character—concentrating on things which are never evident to those who surround him in the novel, but only to its readers—a playwright is somewhat more limited. To be sure, he can give his players soliloquies, or even, as Arthur Miller does in *Death of a Salesman*, dramatize the contents of their minds; but the dramatist is essentially dependent on *signs* for conveying other than direct actions.

The concept of signs is an important aspect of the dramatist's art, a major part of his means for establishing the climate of opinion he desires in his audience. Olson treats *signs* with a show of system, dividing them into "natural" and "artificial." Natural signs include sighs, tears, groans, grimaces, variations in vocal intensity, and the like. Artificial signs depend on some type of convention that is either societal in origin or one established within a given play or genre. As an example of a conventional sign of the first class, Olson cites the funeral wreath or black arm band; the custom of passing the hand before the eyes to denote grief in the Japanese Nō plays applies to the whole genre; and Dr. Rank's calling card is established in *A Doll's House* as a sign that he thinks himself soon to die.

When Olson discusses the relative effectiveness of natural and artificial signs, he says that each is capable of producing the same kind of effect since each may establish opinions; but, since natural signs are universal (a groan in China doesn't differ from its American counterpart), they produce more powerful effects. This is not to say that, under all conditions, natural signs are preferable. For example, in the Nō drama with its aura of serenity, elegance, and beauty, even external events are presented by artificial signs, and deliberately so; for, when the signs are known, they trigger the proper emotions. Then, too, some actions cannot be directly performed on a stage; for example, the actors cannot make long journeys. However, artificial signs can be constructed which will make the fact of a long journey acceptable to an audience.

Olson thinks, in fact, that the Occidental tendency in drama toward realism has tended to make it rely, perhaps too heavily, on natural signs and direct representation. The insistence on realism, if carried too far, results in such literalism as the "unities" of time and place, or, for example, in not allowing deaths to be represented on the stage because the actors do not actually die. Olson thinks that it is especially unfortunate that modern taste has made it seem necessary to model the dialogue of drama on ordinary speech. Because Occidental drama depends on direct representation of action by natural signs, it has, likewise, become dependent on actions with intrinsically high emotional potential. The stylized and serene effects of Oriental drama are rarely exploited by Western dramatists.

We have all along been discussing the strengths and difficulties arising from dramatic manner and how they affect the kinds of actions which can be, or *ought to be,* represented. Certain kinds of external and even some kinds of internal actions are possible on the stage. External actions can be performed directly (an actress can cook or sew, for example), and internal conditions or activities can be exhibited by some form of soliloquy or by natural or artificial signs. Signs, especially artificial ones, extend the range of what is possible in dramatic representation.

II *Plot*

Olson begins the discussion of plot by stating what he considers to be the three basic elements of drama: (1) the human action the play imitates; (2) a scenario which shows what is to be enacted on the stage; (3) the dialogue. From the first of these three, action—together with the actors who perform it—comes plot. I am not again going to state Olson's view of plot other than to repeat that he defines it as "a system of actions of a determinate moral quality." Its importance in drama and in the novel is paramount, as are its analogues in the shorter forms of poetry. In considering plot in drama as morally determinate, all of the factors previously discussed under the headings of "seriousness" and "comicality" have to be brought in. Olson has been, in fact, attacked for his conception of plot by John Holloway because he does not distinguish in its definition between the crude morality of a television Western and that of *King Lear*. Olson's answer to this sort of objection is worth quoting: "I must answer that, in the first place, the question is not one of good and bad plots, but of what is and is not plot. In the second place, a definition of plot must offer universal attributes of plot, ones common to the highest and to the lowest kinds . . . I should be disturbed indeed if my definition did *not* cover the movie melodramas. Besides, the possibility of a crude moral attitude in no way precludes the possibility of a more subtle and refined one." (40-41)

With the definition of plot settled, Olson is in a position to talk of characteristics and kinds of plots. Olson is concerned here only with plots which involve, as he states it, "the activity of two or more characters in a series of situations involving more than one principal event" (41). He calls these *grand plots*, and he says that no work of poetry contains anything more extensive than they. However, it is possible for plots to have, in addition to length, "thickness or thinness," depending on the number of lines of action they involve. Olson points to the plot of Aeschylus' *Agamemnon* as a single line plot, while that of Sophocles' *Oedipus Rex* exemplifies a polylinear plot because it involves the events at Corinth and so on. To qualify as a subplot, a line of action has to be a story in its own right; the actions of Fortinbras and Laertes in *Hamlet* are simply lines of action, but the Gloucester story in *King Lear* is a subplot.

Whether or not lines of action are subplots, they can be related to each other in just three ways. They can diverge, converge, or run parallel; and all these relationships can be used in various ways:

Threatened convergence is one way of obtaining suspense, when the convergence is such as to affect the outcome materially; sudden convergence is one way of obtaining surprise. In *King Lear*, for instance, Albany almost understands the true state of affairs at certain points, and since he has the power to put an end to the villainy, may help Lear's situation: his line threatens to converge with Lear's. The unexpected return of Lovewit in the *Alchemist* is an instance of sudden convergence.

> When lines of action are not merely causally related, . . . they serve to enhance . . . the main line of action, either through resemblance to it or contrast with it. . . . There are more subtle possibilities: the Fortinbras and Laertes lines in *Hamlet* both reflect the main lines as similars and contrast with it, for Fortinbras is like Hamlet a dispossessed prince, and Laertes is like Hamlet the son of a murdered father, and yet both act in sharp contrast to Hamlet. (44)

Olson points out that, because lines of action can be manipulated in so many ways, it is possible to diagram plots after the fashion of E. M. Foster's "patterns." For example, a number of independent lines converging in a point can represent the plot of Wilder's *The Bridge of San Luis Rey*.

Another difference between plots results from the various principles used to unify them. Olson distinguishes four varieties of plot with regard unity, and he exemplifies each. The first type, the "consequential," the plot of "consecutive action," is exemplified by *Macbeth*, which begins with the meeting of the Witches and is centered on the consequences of that meeting which in turn lead causally to the end of the play, and the death of Macbeth.

The second kind of plot is the "descriptive." Wilder's *Our Town* affords a good illustration. This play, Olson thinks, is aimed "at an image of life in a small American town." The completeness of such a plot depends on the completeness of the image it conveys. Incidents in such plots are not causally related but are chosen because they help complete the description of the object under consideration.

Schnitzler's *La Ronde* is used to exemplify what Olson calls the "pattern" plot. He contends that the ten scenes which make up this play contain events which are not causally related but simply form a pattern in which the actors successively change partners as in a round. I agree that, in the sense that *Macbeth* is causally organized, *La Ronde* does not qualify; but I also believe that Schnitzler—in showing life as an empty round in which everyone is, unawares and regard-

less of social position, in much the same situation as everyone
else—is implying a devastating causality. The plot of *La Ronde*,
by the way, seems to me to qualify as symbolic in Olson's
definition. In the play, a view of life is equated with the
activities, or really the *single* activity, in which all its characters
participated. The pattern of which Olson speaks, a definite reality, is an essential part of the symbolic structure because it
too reflects the cyclic view of life the play exhibits. It may
even be that this play is not only symbolic but also didactic.

The last type of plot which Olson designates is the "didactic."
Though Olson doesn't make it clear, this kind of plot would
have to differ from the plots in his original definition in that
it would be dedicated to conveying a doctrine and that doctrine
would determine its quality as in any other didactic poem.
Olson chooses Ibsen's *Ghosts* as his illustration and he says of
it: "The play is a pièce à thèse; the action and the characters
are designed to prove that in a society in which duty is invariably opposed to pleasure, the good must suffer or become
corrupt, while the wicked flourish in hypocrisy" (47).

Still another way in which plots can differ is in terms of
the laws of probability that they employ. Several kinds of
probabilities can be distinguished which operate within the
various forms of drama to control the beings and the objects
they contain. An event can be considered probable if it is
something that commonly happens. Olson who calls this type
"common natural probability," says it is the basis for realistic
and naturalistic plots. Unusual or infrequent happenings can
also be considered probable if the play presents adequate
causes for their occurrence. This type of probability Olson calls
"conditional natural probability."

A third kind of probability results when we recognize that
we are in the presence of great exaggeration because we perceive its underlying truth—that which is exaggerated. To Olson,
this kind of probability, which he labels "hyperbolical," underlies farce.

Still another type of probability results when we accept
the existence of beings who do not, in fact, exist, or of impossible actions on the part of existent beings. All such
probabilities are hypothetical: "If witches, ghosts, and fairies

existed, they *would* do such and such; *if* a dog could talk, he *would* talk like that. This is hypothetical probability, and it underlies all fantasy and stories of the supernatural" (49).

Among other forms of probability are the "conventional" and "emotional." By the first of these Olson means that an audience will accept, without question of probability, well-known or legendary stories, or such standard ingredients of certain forms as the showdown gun duel between the hero and the villain in a Western movie. By the second he means that, if the poet puts his audience in a certain frame of mind, the emotional state which follows makes them tend to accept as probable something they might otherwise question.

A given play can involve more than one kind of probability if shifting probabilities are required by its form. There are many good examples, but a clear one is Shakespeare's *A Midsummer Night's Dream* in which the human and faery worlds operate independently by natural and hypothetical probabilities and, when the two worlds come together in the wood, by both probabilities.

In conclusion, Olson returns to Aristotle and his distinction between simple and complex plots. In "simple" plots, the action moves in a single direction toward either the happiness or the misery of its leading figure. "Complex" plots always involve a change of direction; the protagonist may appear to be heading for good fortune and will then suffer a reversal. Aristotle calls the point at which direction changes the "peripety," and the peripety is usually attended by a discovery: Oedipus discovers, among other things, the true state of his relations with his mother, and his fortunes are completely reversed. The complex plot is superior because it permits the unexpected, and the unexpected is emotionally powerful. Such plots have always at least two forces operating within them; one which seems to carry the action in one direction and another which reverses the first one. Both forces must be probable, but the initial force must seem to dominate in such a way that, when it is reversed, the reversing force can be seen in retrospect to have been the more probable.

Complex plots receive their complications in one of two ways, "continuously" or "incidentally." The word "continuously" is self-explanatory; by "incidentally" Olson means that individual incidents involve complications which are resolved within them and that further development requires new complications of the same order. As examples of continuous complication, which depend more on emotional and other contingent probabilities than natural ones, Olson points to the plots of the great Shakespearean tragedies. Shaw, on the other hand, Olson contends, employs mostly incidental complication and natural probabilities.

III   Incident and Its Relationship to Plot and Character

Plots are made up of incidents, and Olson starts his discussion of them by showing that what is considered an incident in real life depends on the scale in which the events under consideration are placed. In one sense, a major battle is an "incident" in a war which, in turn, might be viewed as an "incident" in the history of man, even though such a battle or war might provide activities enough for dozens of tragedies. On the other hand, an action like rising from a chair, in itself an incident, could be divided into physiological and psychological incidents of great number. The poet, however, cannot view things in his art as he would in real life; he must determine what will constitute an incident within a given work.

The requirement that the poet determine the nature of the incidents in his work imposes certain limitations on him. In the plot of a play, for instance, the "size" of an incident is determined, in one respect, by the emotional effect the work requires of it. Olson is not here talking of the "size" of incidents as represented in a scenario or in terms of the amount of dialogue they involve; he is discussing their complexity as ideas. The general idea of murder, for example, is in itself simple and not evocative of much emotion. However, when such an idea is made specific with a description of the victim, the details of his death, and the characteristics of the murderer, the idea becomes complex and moving. This is not to say, of course, that the "emotional size" of every concept is to be maximized by making its idea as complex as possible in a play. On the contrary, the complexity or "size" (degree of particularity) of the ideas embodied in incidents must be determined by the formal requirements of the play.

Incidents do not merely arouse emotions but must also, if they are to succeed in doing so, contribute to the overall probability of the plot by being probable in themselves, or they must be *made* probable as the result of a process of some sort. As an example of the incident *made* probable, Olson uses the scene in Shakespeare's *Richard III* where Richard convinces Anne that she should marry him though he has just killed her husband. When the probability of an incident is immediately perceptible, its probability, as an idea, is simple in a fashion that is analogous to the simplicity of the general idea of murder cited above. When, however, the probabilities of incidents are not self-evident the "simple" ideas behind them must be analyzed to discover what causes and conditions could make them probable; and these must be made part of them. Olson exemplifies by using a favorite instance of his, the climactic contest between the hero and villain in a melodrama. In cases where the hero is clearly superior in every way, the probability of his victory is self-evident. However, when the villain is tremendously strong, as was Wolf Larsen in London's *The Sea Wolf*, his defeat seems highly improbable; the reasons for it must be produced, as when Larsen becomes blind and his strength is of little value at the crisis. As was the case with emotional impact, the scale of an incident with respect to probability lies in a mean determined by its function in the work.

With the importance of the function of incidents settled, Olson considers the kinds of functions incidents can perform; and he defines four very general varieties. Two of these, he says, relate to the plot; the other two, to the representation. All incidents of the plot are either "essential" or "factorial." By essential Olson means, for example, the elements of Iago's scheme in *Othello*. As an example of a factorial incident, one necessary if the essential ones are to take place, Olson again cites *Othello:* "If Desdemona is to be smothered in bed, she must be there, and Othello must enter the bedchamber; murderer and victim must be brought together" (67).

The two functions of incidents of representation are "either to make the plot or the representation itself more probable or effective; or they are ornamental purely" (68). Again citing *Othello*, Olson says that the major part of Act I is exposition which enhances the plot; but all bridging scenes and transitional passages in any kind of play are included to make the representation more effective. Songs, dances, interludes, parades, and so forth can be purely ornamental, although there are examples to the contrary. Olson cites the ending of Behan's *The Hostage* where the soldier who had apparently died arises and joins in the singing of a song which dispels the gloom of his death.

What has been said of incident applies chiefly to its functions in plots of consecutive action. Essential incidents in descriptive plots (as in *Our Town*) are those which convey aspects of the object under description; they are, in Olson's phrase, "illustrative anecdotes in dramatic form" (70). The scale of an incident in such a play is determined by the importance of what it adds to the description. There is also more freedom for character development in the incidents of descriptive plots since they are not restricted by being required to advance the action. It is easy to see that, in pattern plays, each incident must be dominated by the pattern; and must be approximately the same length as every other; must have similar structure and complexity.

Finally, incidents in didactic plays must act as elements of proof. What Olson says about such incidents adds importantly to what he has said about didactic poetry generally:

There are three kinds of didactic action because there are three kinds of proof: the inductive, the deductive, and the analogical. The inductive action exhibits examples from which we as audience are to generalize. Ibsen's didactic plays are generally of this nature; we are supposed, for instance, to generalize from the examples offered us in *Ghosts*. The deductive action offers generalizations which we are to apply to particulars: for example, *Everyman*, is a dramatic embodiment of generalities; Everyman is not a supposedly particular person like Mrs. Alving. The analogical action always offers some fable or parable which is parallel or proportional to its thesis. The Fox is to the Grapes as the disap-

pointed man to the object of his vain desire. *Aesop's Fables*
or the parables of Jesus illustrate perfectly what I have in
mind, and *Peer Gynt* is a dramatic example. (71)

With this much said about incident and plot, the relationship of incident to character, and character itself are next in
line. Olson's view of character is Aristotelian. "We think,"
says Olson, "of character generally as qualities which dispose
people to a certain kind of conduct; that is, as a capacity
for a certain kind of action" (73). Character, considered this
way, is not the whole personage and everything he does or
suffers; it is only his capacity for moral action. The dramatist
has two tasks: to indicate what that capacity is, and to exhibit
it in action. Character can be exhibited by "incident" as well
as by such formal elements as thought, or, perhaps, by an ex-
pository device of some sort; but incident, unless it has no
other function than to characterize, is clearly part of the plot
and superior to character in a formal sense. As Olson points
out, character, the capacity for moral activity determines in
real life the quality of possible actions. In a play, however,
where plot has been defined as "a system of actions of a certain
moral quality," it is clear that action has priority in a formal
sense and that the characteristics which are assigned to the
play's agents must be such as will permit them to perform the
predetermined actions.

A good deal of confusion has arisen in recent times, a
confusion to which such a fine novelist and critic as E. M.
Forster has contributed, concerning the so-called "novel of
character." Because the formal dominance of plot, or its equivalent, is a key factor in Olson's view of the nature of poetry,
he has addressed himself to the problem presented by works
in which character seems to dominate. His answer, in essence is
quite simple. What is referred to as "character" in such works is
not essentially character at all; it is rather, dominant concern
with internal actions. In the discussion of dramatic and narrative manner, it was pointed out that narrative manner is
better suited to displaying internal actions than dramatic. Even
though this observation is true, internal events tend to dominate
most of Shakespeare's mature plays, and this tendency un-

doubtedly causes Coleridge to think Shakespeare to be much
better at characterization than at plotting.

In other words, Olson says he finds the concept of the novel
or play of character plausible, but only on the assumption that
a plot consists exclusively of external actions. He then goes
on to ask: "Are not incidents in the soul as much incidents
as fist-fights and horse-races? Is the 'secret inner life' not activity? If not, what is it? It cannot consist in that case of thought
or imagination or desires or emotions or even feelings of pleasure and pain; for all these come to be and pass away, are
incidents in a process, are part of mental activity" (76).

With the relationship of incident and character established
and with character defined, Olson returns to a more detailed
analysis of the nature and function of character. He begins by
comparing fictitious characters with real men: (1) a real man
is born with natural capacities; (2) his education and the rep-
etition of certain experiences cause him to develop habits and to
become a certain kind of person with particular moral characteristics; (3) he tends to act in accordance with his character; and
(4) he fills some role in life. When Olson compares the fictious
character with his counterpart in real life, he observes that:

> It would be absurd to say that he was born with certain
> natural capacities. He is an artificial being. But it is unthink-
> able that he should be called upon to do things without
> being given the capacity to do them. Very well: let us give
> him some artificial capacities—ones *appropriate* to what he
> will have to do. Now, he has not formed habits which make
> him into a certain kind of person. We may make him *like* a
> certain kind of person anyway, so that people will have certain
> opinions and feelings about him, just as if he were real. We
> can even invent a fictitious history if necessary, so that he
> may plausibly be what he is. But he still is not really what
> he seems to be; he has not really formed habits according
> to which he will tend to act. What can we do about that?
> Well, we can give him *consistency;* and if he is to act incon-
> sistently, we will make him consistently inconsistent, just as habit
> would in real life. Finally, does he have a function in his
> artificial life? Indeed he has; in fact we invented him for
> just that. . . . He must act in a way *useful* to the plot. (82)

The italicized words—*appropriate, like, consistency,* and *useful*
—are precisely the words Aristotle used to describe the points
which must be observed in the successful construction of
character in chapter 15 of the *Poetics;* the interpretation is
Olson's. As for the function of characters in drama, Olson finds
that, as was the case with incidents, there are four general
ways in which they are employed. Characters are "essential,"
"factorial," "representational," or "ornamental." The protagonist,
of course, is essential; he performs the play's major activities.
Those involved in *factorial incidents* are *factorial;* some, mes-
sengers and the like, may be present only to permit continuity.
Someone who comes on stage to sing a song or to dance is,
most likely, a mere ornament, albeit such an activity may be
the most pleasant thing in a given play.

The possibility that calling all personages in a play characters,
even though most of them are not fully characterized, may be
confusing is what Olson addresses himself to when he considers
"scale" in characterization. Olson thinks that all discussion of
"round" and "flat" characters, and the like, is beside the point.
A character, or more accurately a personage, in a play should be
adequate to the role he fills—nothing more than that and nothing
less. Such essential characters as the protagonist will, in all
likelihood, require full characterization. However, there are
always those in a play who require little or no characterization.
Scale as regards character, is determined, therefore, by the
importance of the character to the plot. Since some of the
people in a play have little or nothing to do with the plot,
the audience needs to know little or nothing about their potential for moral activity.

IV *Representation and Dialogue*

Up to this point, Olson says that he has been talking
conceptually of the elements of drama and that no play comes
into existence until the dramatist has decided what will be
represented on the stage—until he has devised a scenario. The
scenario or representation gives the playwright control over
the actions of the performers; and, consequently, allows him
to control the responses of the audience because what is

represented determines what the audience knows at a given point and, consequently, what they feel. Olson here is reiterating his already familiar theory of the arousal of emotions with special reference to drama. Poets in all sorts of poems employ means appropriate to the forms in which they are working in order to establish the opinions necessary to the emotions they wish to evoke. The dramatist achieves these ends by what he represents on the stage.

Two basic things must be considered in making a decision about whether or not to represent something: probability and emotional effect. In general, a thing should be represented if it enhances either probability or effect; conversely, it should not be represented if representation would weaken either of these. That is the general rule, but often it is necessary to represent things which are nearly neutral. These representations have the function of making the representation itself more effective. Some scenes, says Olson, "permit continuity, facilitate exits and entrances, retain a character on scene for some reason, or simply afford the occasion for some ornament" (93).

To avoid confusion, Olson makes it clear that representation and plot, as he defines the latter, are neither identical nor necessarily coextensive in drama. He contends that the representations in both *Hamlet* and *Othello,* for example, begin well before the plot because each play requires that the audience know certain things and have formed certain attitudes about the characters if the initial incidents of their plots are to have correct effects. In *King Lear,* on the other hand, plot and representation are almost simultaneous.

The more specific problems of what should be represented and of what should not can be discussed hypothetically in terms of the various lines of action a plot contains. In this regard, examples are helpful, both to working playwrights and to critics; and Olson cites many of them:

When the plot is polylinear, there are several possibilities of representation. The main line may be represented, but none of the sub-lines, as in *Oedipus Tyrannus;* or the main line may be represented with all or some of the sub-lines, as in *King Lear;* or the sub-lines may be shown while the

main action takes place off-stage, as in *The Sea-Gull*. A line
can be shown completely or incompletely; for example, the
Laertes line in *Hamlet* can be said to be shown in full, . . .
his going away and coming back are all that is relevant to
the plot. The Fortinbras line, on the other hand, is incompletely shown: we merely get glimpses of him at different
stages in his fortunes. (94)

In judging what is to be represented in the way of main and
sub-lines, the important thing to remember is the overall effect
at which the play is aimed. While, in general terms, the main
line is the chief thing, even it requires special treatment if
the play is aimed at contemplation rather than startling emotional effects. If contemplation is desired, then the emotional
parts of the action must be either suppressed or toned down;
for men are not capable at the same time of both strong feeling and deep reflection. This point is important, for in most
serious work the general intellectual climate of the drama or
novel is ultimately more effective—and, consequently, more af-
fective—than its emotional quality.

What has been said about what should be represented in
a play is barely enough to show the size and number of the
problems the dramatist must solve in making the decision as
to what his scenario will include. Be that as it may, the problems of "how" to represent are perhaps more complex than
those of "what" to represent. At the outset, a problem arises
at the level of incident as to the length and tempo of a given
action; and there are several aspects to this problem. In naturalistic drama, certain actions—for example, putting on a teakettle
—require the same length of time and pacing on the stage
that they would in the kitchen. Certain activities, though not so
demanding as the example just given, nevertheless require
enough time to make them believable. As Olson puts it, "A
portrait . . . cannot be executed in a moment; on the other
hand, it is usually absurd and pointless to represent such
processes of execution at length" (99). He illustrates this last
point by showing how effectively the long process by which
Lady Macbeth has become ill or mad is illustrated in the
single "sleep-walking" scene.

Something can be learned of the "how" of dramatic representation, Olson thinks, by comparing it with its counterpart in narrative, the narrative device; and what Olson says is perhaps as important for the light it throws on the technique of the novel as for its relevance to drama. Basically, novels can be told in the first or third person with the narrator either within or outside the action. With this said, the possibilities of variation of narrative manner can be explored. In cases where the narrator is outside the story—usually the author, though sometimes an observer other than he who has knowledge of the events—the ranges of information he has may be all the way from complete to extremely limited. *The Ambassadors* of Henry James, a good example of the latter, is told from the viewpoint of its protagonist, Strether; James limits himself to knowledge of Strether's thought and activities; and the reader experiences only what he experiences. In *The Idiot*, Dostoyevsky, who limits himself deliberately in the characterization of Prince Myshkin, simply presents the Prince in action and in conversation; he does not analyze his motives or the working of his mind; he lets his speech and action, together with the reactions of those around him, indicate his true nature by implication. Flaubert, in *Madame Bovary*, so focuses the story on Emma that the reader sees and understands no more than she; and he does not realize how inextricably she is involving herself until she does. On the other hand, the author's knowledge may extend to all the characters and events as it does in Fielding and Trollope who, quite often, interject themselves into the narrative to comment. James Joyce extends his knowledge into the unconscious parts of his characters' minds, as does Virginia Woolf.

When the narrator is inside the story, we can usually expect that the information available to him will be limited as a concession to realism. In Fitzgerald's *The Great Gatsby*, we are treated to the process by which the narrator, Nick Carraway, learns Gatsby's story; and, at the end, we and he have information which neither of us had at the beginning. The way in which Melville limits his narrator, Ishmael, in *Moby Dick* —not to mention the limitations imposed by Melville's occasional simulation of dramatic manner—heightens the mystery and power of Captain Ahab.

These are enough examples to show that the narrative device by means of which a novel is told is an important consideration and that a great variety of treatments of it is possible. The same thing is true in drama even to the extent that a narrator can be employed, as one is in the person of the stage manager in *Our Town*. Other variations of representation are also possible in drama: the introduction of a chorus, or other commentator, or of a play within a play, and so on. The most important difference between the use of complex devices of manner in the novel and in the drama is that the novel is in this respect, much more flexible than the drama. Novels of the highest seriousness, Joyce's *Ulysses* or Conrad's *Chance*, achieve much of their power from complex narrative techniques. Olson believes, however, that—while a representative device like the stage manager in *Our Town* has certain advantages (there are no problems about exits and entrances, for examples; the narrator simply calls and dismisses the character as he needs them)—the greatest drama has never employed anything of its kind. "Shakespeare," says Olson, "never uses the representative devices which appeal to Pirandello and Wilder; he is content with simply arranging the representation so that scene by scene we take the view he wishes us to take" (103). In the mature Shakespeare there is no gimmickry to diminish the inexorable continuity of the action and the aura of high seriousness.

As a lead into the discussion of the role of dialogue in drama, Olson reapproaches signs to analyze them in relation to their powers of implication. Signs, in this sense, are either complete, incomplete, or multiple. A complete sign is one from which a single inference may be drawn; an incomplete one must be joined with others before its implications can be understood; and a multiple sign is one from which many inferences can be made. Olson illustrates from *Othello*:

> Brabantio's "How! The Duke in Council!" is a complete sign, simply implying surprise. Roderigo's first speech, "I take it much unkindly . . . that thou shouldst know of this," tells us nothing beyond what it directly says; we must know more to see what it implies. This is an incomplete sign. Othello's "Keep

up your bright swords, for the dew will rust them," is a
multiple sign. We can infer from it all the better part of
his character.([105])

Olson then explains that Othello's speech is in reply to Bra-
bantio's insult and command to attack him. Such a mild reply
shows his bravery, the bravery of one who is so familiar with
danger that he has developed the habit of courage—a courage
which enables him to joke gently in the face of danger. Swords
are out, but they *will not* be used; if they are not put away,
they will rust.

In addition to completeness, or lack of it, signs are particular or general. Particularity derived from specificity (someone actually crying on the stage when we know the seriousness of his anguish) is more moving than generality (tears
without the explanation). Olson thinks the emotional flatness
of much of later seventeenth and eighteenth-century drama
in England results from the use of too many general signs.
He contends that it is easy to predict what Dryden's Antony or
Cleopatra will do, or what they will not do. "I cannot imagine,"
he says, "that Dryden's Antony would tease Cleopatra as she
helped him with his armor, or that Dryden's Cleopatra would
'hop forty paces through the public streets,' or be breathless
if she did. They are not alive enough for that" (107).

Signs can also be ambiguous or clear. They are clear when
the implication is just what the audience takes it to be;
they are ambiguous when more than one conflicting inference
is possible (a man running from a house where a murder has
been committed presents many possibilities for inference). In
any event, Olson concludes, signs are devices, and they must
be used in such a way as to maximize the effects required
by the plot.

It should be clear at this point that, in the discussion of
signs, much of what can be said of dialogue has already been
said. Dialogue is a chief means of conveying signs to the
audience (not every blush or paleness is visible to the audience,
but a character can observe them and point them out):
"Dialogue offers us many signs, and so sets action and char-

acter before us, vividly and convincingly. Besides that, if it is long, it makes the scene long, so it is clearly related to the important business of representative scale. It makes possible the representation of many things—complicated thought, delicate shades of passion, for example, that would not otherwise be possible" (112).

Everything in Olson's position on the role of diction in mimetic poetry applies to his view of dialogue, and those portions dealing with the function of language simply as language need not be repeated. However, he also contended that to consider speech as action is to consider it most importantly. In this respect, the lyric is much more limited than the drama, for the lyric poet can display only as much action, character, thought, and feeling as can be made understandable in a relatively short space. The dramatist, however, has an extensive context of actions in which a given speech fits and from which it derives the better part of its power. In another place, which can be cited to enforce the point here, Olson cited Lear's "Pray you, undo this button" speech as an example of the emotional force which can be packed into such a simple request. In isolation, the speech would have little or no power to evoke feelings; but, in the context of Lear's character and situation, it is devastating. The dramatic context is paramount even in speeches where great beauty is present in the imagery, figures, and rhythm. A dialogue between the King and Banquo[2] is a case in point:

> *King.* This castle hath a pleasant seat. The air
> Nimbly and sweetly recommends itself
> **Unto our gentle senses**
> *Banquo.*   This guest of summer,
>
> The temple-haunting martlet, does approve
> By his lov'd mansionry that the heaven's breath
> Smells wooingly here. No jutty, frieze,
> Buttress, nor coign of vantage, but this bird
> Hath made his pendent bed and procreant cradle.
> Where they most breed and haunt, I have observ'd
> The air is delicate.

There is indeed a magic in this description of Macbeth's castle

which would be effective even if we did not know more of
Duncan and Banquo than we do. Under the circumstances of
their impending murders, however, their speeches so revelatory
of their characters and of their appreciation of the beauty of the
place in which they are to die, are tremendously ironic and
moving. Nor is the effect diminished by the talk of procreation
and birth; the condemned have no inkling of doom.

V *Tragedy in Our Time*

Before it is possible to talk of tragedy in modern times, it
is necessary to say what makes a play tragic in any time. Olson,
of course, accepts Aristotle's definition of tragedy. In so doing,
he rules out such stock ideas as that the characters must have
a high social status or that tragedies must always end un-
happily. It is possible to crowd the stage with kings and to
kill them all without achieving the tragic effect. As far as
Aristotle is concerned, comedy and tragedy are like, except in
one essential: the quality of their objects of imitation. The
comic imitates actions and agents who are either unimportant
or ridiculous. Tragedy depends on the ability of the poet to
put before us something supremely serious and important.
We take seriously, Olson reiterates, "Whatever can importantly
affect our happiness and misery; whatever can give great
pleasure or pain, mental or physical; whatever similarly affects the happiness or pleasure of those for whom we have
some concern, or of a good number of people, or of people
whom we take to be of considerable worth; or whatever involves a principle upon which all such things depend; or
anything that bears a sufficient resemblance to these, or a
sufficient relation" (241-42).

A serious play, like any serious poem, must support an
intellectual climate invulnerable to disbelief. "Invulnerable
to disbelief," means simply that, when a play proposes an
important state of affairs as possibly true, and, as a consequence of its truth, as possibly productive of joy or misery,
the possibility must be able to withstand the most penetrating
analysis. Many great dramatists from Aeschylus to Arthur
Miller, as well as a number of novelists and lyricists, have, in

Olson's opinion, achieved this kind of seriousness. Olson thinks Miller's *The Crucible* is one of the closest modern approximations of tragedy because of the importance of the moral issues it involves. John Proctor's refusal to live unless he can retain his integrity involves a moral position the truth of which is invulnerably possible to anyone of normal perceptiveness. Further, Miller puts Proctor into the position where he must make his decision by a series of probable causes and effects. An audience which watches the plot of *The Crucible* unfold cannot but wonder at Proctor's moral strength and at the rightness of his decision; and the spectators cannot but have an awareness and fear that they might not do so well under similar circumstances, Some may even realize that such circumstances are always present and that integrity and dignity cannot be maintained in any life without courage.

Where Miller has succeeded in seriousness and tragic effect, most modern playwrights, Olson thinks, have failed. He cites O'Neill's *Mourning Becomes Electra* as an example of a work which fails of seriousness. Olson thinks that O'Neill's treatment of Aeschylus' *Oresteia* debases its seriousness, not because of the change of locale or modernization, but because the whole conception has been weakened:

> Orin and Lavinia are . . . debasements of their proto-
> types. Orestes commits actual matricide, in horror and revul-
> sion, under divine direction; Orin is a psychotic, moved by
> unconscious incestuous desires; and his guilt in his mother's
> death is merely fancied. Electra suffers dishonor, privation,
> and oppression, sees her people laboring under a tyranny, and her
> father's murderers flourishing unpunished; she acts to restore
> justice. Lavinia is a girl cheated of her love by her mother. (24)

Olson thinks that the general lack of seriousness in modern drama stems at least partly from its commitment to realism. One of the results has been the disappearance of verse from the drama. The failure to versify in itself is not crucial to seriousness, but it is a symptom of something more basic:

> Verse has practically disappeared from modern drama; despite

certain notable exceptions, it is a prose drama. And the prose
—again with certain exceptions—is no greatly varied prose.
On the contrary it has shown a tendency to become more and
more like ordinary speech, or rather, more and more like
the ordinary speech of the man who is a little less than the
ordinary. The drama has increasingly sought to be articulate
in the language of the inarticulate; and because it has done
so, it has had to confine itself to such subject matter as its
language might permit. The language of the inarticulate does
not permit the expression of subtle or profound thought or
emotion; consequently drama has had to forego the subtler
and profounder thoughts and emotions. And since language
and thought and emotion enter into the subtler expressions
of character, drama has had to forego the latter as well. (224)

Olson is not beating the drum for a return to versified drama,
though he thinks that verse is, on certain dramatic occasions,
more appropriate than prose. But he is saying what we said at
the beginning of this section: that seriousness is a quality of
the objects of imitation. Seriousness can only result when men
with truly human capacities for thought and feeling are depicted performing actions, either mental or physical, the consequences of which are of supreme importance to the happiness
or misery of all. The discoveries Hamlet makes about men,
about the world, and, perhaps by inference, about the universe
are terrifyingly possible; also possible is the grand stoicism with
which he learns to accept these truths.

CHAPTER 5

Practical Criticism: The Drama

Elder Olson's work as a practical critic, though limited in bulk, serves at least four useful functions: (1) it is elaborative of his theories of the poetic arts in many directions; (2) it is an illustration of his theories in operation; (3) it is a model for practical critics; and (4) it illuminates the writings of some of the greatest poets both ancient and modern. The material in this chapter is drawn from chapters VII through X of *Tragedy and the Theory of Drama*.[1]

I *Aeschylus*

Olson has made it clear on several occasions[2]—though, if he hadn't, it could have been inferred from his theory of plot —that the translator of a work, seeing that diction is the least important of a poem's formal elements, must first be concerned to translate its more fundamental elements, plot and character, and be only subsidiarily concerned with the original language's rhythms, sounds, and syntax. As concerns these last, the important thing is to make them as appropriate to plot and character in the second language as they were in the original. Olson makes the basic point by commenting that even a play like *Macbeth*, in which the beauty of the language is so important, can be translated successfully because the dramatic conception which underlies it can be recreated in any language.

There are, then, more fundamental things to translation than language; but, in the case of Aeschylus, the Greek and the English in themselves tend, perhaps, to present more problems than the fundamentals. These problems arise from the structural differences in the two languages and from diverse cultural en-

vironments in which ancient Greek was, and modern English
is, spoken. Olson cites several translations of a single line from
the *Oresteia* and observes that, in spite of quite wide differences, each is an adequate translation of the meaning of the
original; that all the translators are excellent Greek scholars;
and that one of them, Robert Browning, is among the greatest
poets. The point Olson is making is that, while there are a
number of fairly effective translations possible, each translator
confronts the same, ultimately insoluble, problem: "What constitutes the true English equivalent of the original in *every
aspect*" (174). The best any translator can achieve is a kind
of compromise. Aeschylus' style, as Olson describes it, is "a
dignified, and exalted one." In casting about for an English
equivalent in dignity and exaltation, the translator is apt to
select the style of Milton or that of the King James Old Testament. To make a translation in either of these styles, or similarly foreign ones, is, Olson thinks, to import something into
Aeschylus which has nothing to do with his work.

On the other hand, literal translations are too tame. What
must have been exciting quantitative verse in Greek translates
in English, even when versified, into very flat language. Perhaps
the very difference in the genius of the two languages which
permits quantity in Greek verse, and makes attempts at it in
English stilted, is responsible. At any rate, Olson advises translators that "The plain English isn't exciting enough, we must
use some literary cosmetics, brighten Aeschylus up a bit, even
though in the end we are likely to see, not his face, but our
paint" (175). The compromise translation would seem to
consist in certain modest embellishments to literal translations
as preferable to something completely foreign to the original.

Cultural differences present similar problems to the translator. Olson thinks, for example, that "differences of convention make it impossible for us to feel the deep religious horror
of the Greeks at regicide, parricide, and incest, horrible as we
may still consider these" (176). The problem is not so much
the words themselves as the conceptions which underlie them.
The translator, where local attitudes are of importance to the
emotional effect of the play, cannot always successfully translate them literally, but must often seek similars about which

the audience for whom he is translating feels strongly.

Olson thinks that the kind of development which English drama has undergone over the centuries has conditioned us to expect a good deal of action, mostly external, and, in consequence, plots with many episodes and many lines of action. Olson calls the technique of the plays admired most today *aggregation,* and he contrasts this technique with what he calls *isolation.* Oriental artists, he contends, have always employed isolation both in drama and in interior decoration. Olson cites the instance of the astonishment of an Englishman "entering a house in Penang and finding in it no article of furniture except a large vase on a stand; exquisite, it illuminated and dominated the room, and afforded scope for contemplation" (178). Recalling my own days in Japan, I remember many austere rooms in which the eye was drawn to a single beautiful *kaketsu* or flower arrangement primarily because there was nothing else to offer a distraction.

To recognize that Aeschylus used the technique of isolation is essential to understand him. Olson does not think, in spite of the virtues of the technique (by the way, he does not prefer it to *aggregation*), that Aeschylus adopted it by choice; rather, the state of drama in his time caused him to use it. Greek drama began, as Olson sees it, in choric poems with some dramatic elements; and drama proper only became possible when "distinct dramatic entities" were impersonated. Homer, he says, did this in his epics, and there is evidence that other minstrels had also done so before him; but the practice first entered the drama only "when the *choragus* or chorus leader, in the performance of the dithyramb, impersonated the god and indulged in a brief passage of dialogue with the chorus" (179).

Before Aeschylus, Greek drama under Thespis and Phyrnichus had developed to the point where serious actions were depicted, where the diction was elevated, and where the chorus had been divided into separate groups and in effect into separate dramatic entities. Aeschylus, who added a second actor to this essentially choral drama, opened up the possibilities for more extensive actions and for a dialogue that really subserves the plot.

Olson describes the action of the *Oresteia* as "three short sequences of incidents centering about a principal event" (180). Each of these sequences, he thinks, is isolated in the sense that none of them draws its power from a dramatic context. The action of *Agamemnon* affords good illustration; it is, Olson says, "one single deed, the murder of the king" (181). Olson then compares the action of *Agamemnon* with a typical Shake-spearean action. While *Agamemnon* presents a succession of incidents, even as *Hamlet* does, there is a basic difference. The incidents in *Hamlet* succeed one another causally and are, for the most part, what Olson has called *essential* incidents. *Agamemnon* contains only one essential incident, the murder; the other incidents are simply dramatized circumstances of it.

The single central deed of *Agamemnon* is what Aristotle calls the *tragic deed*. Such a deed, as Aristotle defines it, destroys the life or happiness of its victim and is committed by someone from whom he would not expect it, at a time when it seems remote. Certainly, with minor qualification, Agamemnon's murder is such a pitiful event. In spite of the pity evoked by Agamemnon's death, Olson thinks it is aroused, not for Agamemnon's sake primarily, but in order to increase our awareness of the terrible deed itself, Clytemnestra's deed: "The *Agamemnon* is Clytemnestra's play; the king is merely the victim. It is not so much the matter of his *dying* as of her *killing* that engrosses us" (183). The terrible act with its definite moral quality is the plot of the play.

In order for the deed to be nothing more than a simple horror, Aeschylus had to contrive characters, an agent and a patient, whose qualities would indicate, in part, the seriousness of it. Both Clytemnestra and Agamemnon are conceived regal-ly. To Clytemnestra, Aeschylus assigns a number of motives for the murder; and some of them, as Olson notes, are rather base: her desire to keep her lover; her wish to maintain power; and, one that Olson doesn't mention (though it may have been, I think, crucial), her jealousy of Cassandra—the possibility that Cassandra was Agamemnon's mistress would dull the element of revenge in her affair with Aegisthus. More noble motives are Clytemnestra's feeling that she must obtain justice for the death of Iphigenia (Olson doesn't, in his emphasis on Clytemnestra, make enough of Agamemnon's role in sealing his own doom, including the act of *hybris* in walking on the purple carpet as well as in the murder of his daughter, etc.); the fact that she thinks that she will remove the curse from the house of Atreus; and her conviction that her rule, unlike that of Agamemnon with its "war for a whore," will be just.

As Olson says, however, Clytemnestra's motives are best understood within the framework of her character. He sees her as a wicked woman, but one whom it is impossible not to respect and admire. She has tremendous strength and fierce passions. She is always under control, a control made remarkable because it is present even in her exultation in the act of killing Agamemnon. She feels refreshed, as does the corn when it rains, when his blood spatters her. In spite of her essentially masculine personality, one which the chorus comments on so ironically, she uses her femininity to utmost advantage: no one, least of all a loving husband, would suspect a woman of the deed she contemplates. In the crucial scenes where Agamemnon must be convinced, or the plan will fail, she is most wilily feminine.

Clytemnestra, like her husband, is a serious character; and her deed, appropriately, is a serious one, the seriousness of which is augmented by the way in which Aeschylus has represented it and because, as Olson observes, "It comes out of great and prolonged calamities and is to eventuate in more. It involves the happiness of a nation. It involves a principle of justice upon which man's conduct must depend if he is to be man and not beast . . . Man as an individual cannot know justice and cannot pursue it; for men and gods there must be law" (188).

Olson thinks that much of the effect of *Agamemnon* depends on making Clytemnestra's character mysterious. Her character is really ambiguous until the final revelation which comes, consequently, as a surprise. In order to make this effect possible, the audience has to be kept in the same state of knowledge as the chorus. Aeschylus could not represent any scene which would too clearly expose Clytemnestra's character. Olson thinks that the news of the fall of Troy could not be announced directly to her because she would have either to exhibit her true feelings, and dispel all mystery at once, or to conceal them, and produce a lifeless scene. The watchman scene, with its telegraphic fires, and its own interest, makes an effective compromise.

But the scenes in which Clytemnestra *does* appear are much more to the point. In her first entrance, she announces the news of the victory to the Chorus of Elders. Olson compares this scene with Mark Antony's speech over Caesar's body. It must be represented directly because, unless she is shown effectively as doing it, it would be improbable that she could deceive everyone and also change the public mind. Here she practices all her feminine tricks, and the scene prepares for her success with Agamemnon by exposing, as Olson puts it, "all the traits which imply what she is and what she will do, without our being able to draw the startling but obvious inference" (190). The scene with the herald is preparation for Agamemnon's return, and the Chorus is again unable to see through Clytemnestra. If it had, Agamemnon would have been saved. There are several points in the play at which the line of action leading to the murder threatens to converge with an implicit line which could save him. As Olson notes, these two lines never converge; there is, consequently, no complication, but suspense is strengthened by the threat of convergence.

These near convergences are even more threatening in Agamemnon's arrival scene where the slightest suspicion on his part would ruin Clytemnestra's plan. Even after Clytemnestra persuades him to enter the palace, Cassandra's refusal to go along is ominous for Clytemnestra's success:

> Agamemnon has entered the palace, and Cassandra does not follow him despite the commands and imprecations of Clytemnestra. She remains silent—a deliberate reversion on the poet's part to the older technique of having one person remain mute while two speakers discourse—but what an employment of a mute! . . . A significant, a portentous, a terrible silence —the most dreadful silence in all drama. Clytemnestra herself, in all her unshakeable calm, is shaken by that silence: for the first time her mask falls; she discloses something of the proud, arrogant woman she is; she withdraws. (191)

The scene which follows shows Cassandra calling upon Apollo

in what to the chorus seem mad and disordered phrases (how appropriate her wildness to the murder preparations within; how inappropriate to have shown these preparations) and, at the end, her entrance to the place of death followed by Agamemnon's terrible and enlightening death cry. Olson is right to consider the scenes just described among the most dramatic possible, but he is also right to say that even their power is overshadowed in the final scene where Clytemnestra reveals her true character in her exaltation at the murder and in her intention to govern well. Neither the Chorus nor the audience is prepared completely (the representation has been too skillful in what it concealed) for such a revelation.

II *Shakespeare*

As was the case with Aeschylus, Olson discusses Shakespeare's art by thoroughly analysing one play, *King Lear*, from the working dramatist's point of view. As *Agamemnon* was an example of the technique of "isolation," *Lear*, with its consequential and polylinear plot, is an example of the technique of "aggregation." Adopting the point of view of the *working dramatist*, Olson thinks, makes it easier to answer the kinds of questions which have been asked about the play: "Why does Lear devise that 'silly trick,' as Coleridge calls it, of demanding that the daughters profess their love? Why does Cordelia refuse? Why is the plot so complicated? Why are there so many characters? Why the parallel story of Gloucester? Why must Gloucester's eyes be put out on stage? Why should Lear and Cordelia die?" (196-97).

Olson hastens to make it plain that, in adopting the working dramatist's point of view, he is not going to expose the "secret workings" of Shakespeare's mind which are individual with him. "All," he says "that we shall see is a dramatist who has one general problem which involves a whole complex of special problems and who tries, like any other artist, to solve them in the best possible way" (198). One reviewer[3] has pointed out that the critical technique employed here is similar to Poe's description of the writing of "The Raven" in *The Philosophy of Composition.* The technique is often, though not exclusively, used

by Olson and others of the Chicago critics. It has the virtue
of the ingenious in holding our attention, but it should, I think,
only be used where a less precious frontal attack would be
less effective. Be that as it may, the working dramatist's point
of view is an advantageous one.

The general problem is how to make an old story with a
very obvious moral, "actions speak louder than words," into
something tragic. The solution of Shakespeare is to replace the
generalized king, almost an abstraction in the older versions,
with a real person; someone particularized enough to engage
the sympathies. The *events* of the older tale can be retained,
but the quality of seriousness will be added as the events
become the *acts* of a serious character. And what, asks Olson,
must the characteristics of Lear be if the play is to be tragic?
In answering, Olson is one again with Aristotle: Lear cannot
be a perfect man and, hence, above pity, nor can he be someone whose misfortunes are deserved. The act of banishing Cordelia can only be a tragic act if it results from "compulsion or
passion or incomplete knowledge; and though it is not a
right action, it must *seem* right action—that is it cannot be a
piece of *knowing* injustice—to Lear at the time he commits
it" (200). The character of Lear must be ennobled, and he
must be shown to act in all cases from causes appropriate to
the noble.

Olson then examines the action of the play in order to clarify
what he has been contending. He begins by examining the
reasons Lear divides the kingdom:

> Why does Lear divide the kingdom? Because he is without
> male issue; consequently he has no real successor; conse-
> quently he wishes to avert war between the pretenders after
> his death by an equal division. Why does he abrogate
> authority? Because he is becoming too old to rule, and
> because he thinks that if the division is made in his lifetime
> and established as a going concern, there is less chance of
> war. And what is the point of his demanding the public pro-
> fession of love? Well, in *part* it is this: if Lear is giving up
> his authority and still wants security and dignity, he can
> only trust to their love; and his insistence upon their public
> profession of it is an attempt to have it witnessed as a formal

part of the compact of the delivery of property and power. (201)

Olson has italicized "part" because something more must be said. That something more, as it turns out, involves what I think is a major contribution to Shakespearean criticism, a brief but penetrating analysis of Shakespeare's conception of *hamartia,* the tragic mistake. In Greek tragedy the tragic situation is brought about by the gods or the fates or, as in the *Oresteia,* by a curse in which the tragic figure's *actions* (free choices) involve him. The Romans, Olson says, if Seneca is typical, do not allow moral agency at all; their characters simply suffer a certain fate. Shakespeare, however, "has worked out his own formula for . . . the tragic mistake; and so far as I know, it is one peculiar to him" (202). Hamlet, he says, is a scholar and philosopher by training and temperament; he is a speculative thinker, not a person given to action. Yet he *must act* in a practical situation in which speculation is defeating. Othello, Olson continues, is a general; and a good general must depend on the advice and trust of his lieutenants. Othello is put in a position where to take the advice of his subordinate is destructive. Coriolanus, likewise, is a general; and he is placed in a position where, instead of commanding support, he must request it. Macbeth's courage has lifted him to eminence, but his wife plays on his courage to drive him to murder the king. To Olson, "In brief the thing is this: a character of conspicuous virtues and abilities, who has distinguished himself through them in one sphere, is thrown suddenly into a sphere of action in which to exercise them—and he *must* exercise them—is to invoke catastrophe. A far sadder notion than the Greek: we fall, not through our vices merely, but even through our virtues" (202).

"Lear," Olson continues, "is a feudal lord . . . thrown into a domestic sphere where the laws of feudality do not operate, for he is abrogating the authority on which feudality depends" (203). Lear, says Olson, is simply performing the feudal act of demanding a profession of loyalty from his vassals as a condition of turning over his authority and property. It is, as a feudal lord who desires to keep his kingship, the only way he knows. To support his view, Olson cogently points to the legal-istic phrasing of the speeches in which Lear responds to the positive replies of Goneril and Regan. If Lear is mistaken, he is so in the pursuit of a kingly principle.

Cordelia, a favorite daughter, does not grasp the feudal principle behind Lear's action; and he, in turn, cannot under-stand why she will not accede to what he thinks to be necessary conditions. She does not realize that he is not acting in this case as a father but as a king. And, as Olson puts it, "the familial and the feudal do not mix . . . The one demands forms and contracts; the other depends wholly upon trust. A feudal lord may demand the exclusive loyalty of his vassal; a father can make no such demand upon his daughter's affection" (204). To do as Lear did is, Olson contends, to sin against love; in order to expiate his sin, he must discover what love really means through being deprived of it. "Without love, and benevolence and the humane feelings," Olson argues, "man becomes a beast, justice and law become empty forms, author-ity becomes mere force, and the world becomes the nightmare of cannibalistic nature where all prey on all. Lear has driven love away for the sake of empty forms; he must fall into that night-mare world and suffer in it" (205).

If Lear must suffer, his must not be simple physical suffer-ing. Lear, says Olson, has to suffer because of the principle in-volved; for "Each of Shakespeare's great tragic heroes pays in his own personal coin: the courageous Macbeth in moral terror, the intellectual Hamlet in doubt and confusion; and the proud, just, affectionate Lear must pay in the suffering of humilia-tion, injustice, and the privation of affection" (206). His suffer-ing eventuates in madness. Olson notes that Shakespeare's Lear is the only one who goes mad; he is the only one profoundly enough conceived to be capable of such an ultimate torment. The gradual realization of the full implications of his act are too great for him to bear.

Olson's discussion of the reasons for the "unhappy" ending of *Lear*, as is the case with so much of his analysis, has appli-cations to, and grows out of, Shakespeare's tragic art. Olson contends that the death-filled endings of Shakespeare's great tragedies *seldom* are a requirement of their antecedent action.

He asks, for example, "What in the plot necessitates that Emilia should come too late to save Desdemona? Hamlet's death-wound, poisoned though the sword is, is a mere possibility of combat" (207). Likewise, Cordelia's defeat at the end of *Lear*, is not inevitable, nor would it have been impossible for Edmund to speak in time to save her.

If the endings of these plays are no more probable than other alternatives, another kind of necessity must be found for them. Olson thinks the necessity is an emotional one; and, in the course of discussing it, he gives a good account of Aristotle's remarks about *catharsis:* "In every true tragedy the audience is compelled to transcend from a *lower* set of moral values to a higher; it is compelled to fear and pity, for instance, only to acknowledge in the end that in a higher judgment there are worse evils than those it has been fearing and pitying; and by confronting that great misery it has learned, momentarily at least, something of the great conditions upon which human happiness truly depends, and something of the high dignity of which man is capable" (208). A *Lear* with a happy ending is one without the tragic effect; only Shakespeare's version, in the death of a Lear who has learned in the most absolute way the relationship of love to human happiness, achieves that effect.

Olson, who turns next to the lesser characters, thinks the character of Cordelia must be a simple one. She performs the functions of providing the object for Lear's love, and she furnishes the occasion for the lesson he learns when he rejects that love. Olson does not, as so many critics do, think Cordelia "obstinate"; instead, she is only *"persistently candid"* because of the depth of her affection and her personal integrity. Cordelia is her father's daughter in both these respects. Though their misunderstanding is complete, the characteristics which motivate each are very much alike.

Olson thinks that a high principle is involved in the characterizations of Goneril and Regan; they must be truly evil if the play is to have its fullest effects, and Shakespeare makes them evil by making them so completely self-interested that they are incapable of good; the truly self-interested will go to any ends to achieve what they consider, however mistakenly, that self-interest to be.

Olson next justifies Shakespeare's inclusion of the Gloucester subplot. Its justification depends on certain peculiarities of the plot of *Lear* as compared with other Shakespearean plots. The plot of Lear begins immediately with the tragic act, the banishment of Cordelia; it, therefore, can be concerned only with the consequences of that act. In *Othello,* on the contrary, the tragic act occurs near the end. Moreover, Lear's initial act deprives him of the power to act again. Almost all of Shakespeare's heroes can do something. Hamlet, Macbeth, Coriolanus, Othello are not powerless. All Lear can do is suffer. He cannot go to Cordelia; to do so would reduce his stature. Someone to act for him is required.

Seeing that Goneril and Regan both act on the principle of self-interest, a device which would pit self-interest of one against that of the other would be very useful. A plot unrelievedly exhibiting the greater and greater suffering of, and danger to, Lear would be tiring. Something must be invented to break into the main line of action. Something "to *reinforce* it; to raise false hopes for . . . Lear again and again; for when the audience has been led to hope for the tragic figure, and that hope is frustrated, it feels more forcibly than ever the agony of his plight" (211). The Gloucester subplot, right down to supplying Edmund for Goneril and Regan to fall out over, satisfies all these requirements. Moreover, the Gloucester line involves the same moral issues as the main line; but since it does not have the same tragic powers, it does not compete with it.

Olson's final concern with *King Lear* is with its representation. Shakespeare, he says, wants to arouse sympathy as strongly as he can for Lear, and he knows that sympathy is enhanced if the audience is misled into thinking him unsympathetic at first only to discover it was mistaken. The device Shakespeare uses to achieve this result is what Olson calls "ambiguous action": "He [Shakespeare] invents actions for Lear, in the early part of the play, which on first sight look quite different from what they really are: his demand that his daughterss profess their love publicly is . . . the supreme example. His banishment of Cordelia is in any case a dreadful thing, but it is not a vicious moral action; it is a piece of folly, excusable in view of his character and his career" (213).

Some critics have criticized *King Lear* for not having a long exposition like that of *Macbeth, Hamlet, or Othello;* but the answer is simple and clear: in those plays, a good deal of information is prior to the full effectiveness of the plot; in *Lear,* the contrary is true—the full power of the plot depends on the audience's not knowing too much.

Like the character of their father, the characters of Goneril and Regan are unfolded gradually. Lear's resentment of them develops, as does that of the audience, as they become better known. Also, the blinding of Gloucester, Olson thinks, must be represented because it shows without question what Regan is capable of; what she might have done, *a fortiori*, to Lear.

In his final paragraph on *King Lear,* Olson comments very briefly on the role of Albany who, at the end, hands out justice. Albany is always able to stop the events whenever he wishes. He does not do so, says Olson, because, like the audience, he tends to view Lear unfavorably at first and only gradually learns the truth.

Brief as Olson's treatment of *King Lear* is, it plays a bright new light over it. His remarks on Lear, together with such aspects of his theory as he did not apply to it (the concepts of probability and diction among them), indicate the kind of detailed analyses which would be possible, not of *King Lear* alone, but of the entire Shakespearean canon.

III *Racine*

Though Olson calls his chapter on Racine, *Phèdre,* it is as much a continuation of his examination of Shakespeare as anything. Olson thinks that Racine has made a contribution to dramatic art; but, to illustrate what that contribution is, he compares Racine's technique with Shakespeare's. In contrast to the aggregative technique of Shakespeare, Racine employs *isolation,* not as the Greeks did from the necessity imposed by the state of the drama in their time, but through choice of it for its values. If the *plot* of a Shakespearean tragedy is compared with that of one of Racine's, the former is immediately seen to be more extensive than that of the latter.

Olson is not here simply saying that Racine observes the

unities of time and place but that Shakespeare includes far more incidents. In fact, he observes the Gloucester *subplot* of *King Lear* has more incidents than the *plot* of *Phèdre*. A closer look reveals, moreover, that important scenes in Shakespeare are compounded of a multitude of minor incidents, as in the scene from *Lear* in which Gloucester is blinded:

> Cornwall, to whom Edmund has betrayed his father, asks Goneril to hasten to tell Albany that the French army has landed, and orders Gloucester apprehended. Regan wants to hang him at once. Goneril suggests the plucking out of his eyes. Cornwall silences both and sends Edmund along with Goneril. Oswald comes to tell of Lear's escape to Dover. Cornwall decides the fate of Gloucester, implying he will not be killed. Gloucester is brought in. He pleads but is bound. Accused of treason, he denies it; Regan tears hairs from his beard: he rebukes her. Now he is interrogated. His answers enrage Cornwall and Regan; Cornwall puts out one eye. An old servant of Cornwall's rebels as Cornwall is about to put out the other. They fight, Cornwall is wounded; Regan stabs the servant from behind, killing him. The other eye is out. Gloucester in agony calls his son Edmund; Regan brutally discloses that it was Edmund who betrayed him. Gloucester realizes that he has unjustly suspected Edgar. Gloucester is thrust out of doors to wander blind. Cornwall announces his wound, withdraws to die. The servants discuss the atrocity they have witnessed; they decide to provide medicaments for him and to get Edgar, whom they know as poor Tom, to guide him. (222-23)

In contrast with the blinding scene, the essential scene in which *Phèdre* reveals her love for her stepson contains only that incident. Her nurse questions her, and she replies.

Shakespeare's scenes are more complex than Racine's in several additional ways. Shakespeare's scenes are relatively heavily populated with personages who are doing something. "Our attention," Olson says, "may not be upon them but they are still alive and there, and responding in their own ways to whatever is happening" (224). To illustrate, he examines the Gloucester scene again: Regan, the direct one, wants Gloucester hanged;

the vicious Goneril wants his eyes gouged out; Cornwall is making a decision; Edmund must remain silent since his treachery has put him where he wants to be; and the servant who wounds Cornwall is also silent. If each character is examined, Shakespeare's vision of his response to the situation is evident.

Olson compares this scene with the one in *Phèdre* where Hippolyte reveals to Aricie that he loves her. There are others present, but Racine gives no indication at all as to how they react. As Olson observes, "the French playwright's scenes are duets *alternando;* one character speaks, the other responds. Others are mute. Shakespeare's scene are duets and trios and quartets and quintets, whole symphonies even" (225). Further, Shakespeare's scenes are *"highly circumstantial."* They are set in definite places with definite characteristics and at definite times. Olson asks us to recall how much we know about Macbeth's castle, how precisely we know what time of day it is in *Othello,* or, in general, how Shakespeare's characters are dressed, what kind of things are about them, and how they react to those things. In *Phèdre* we are told that the scene is Troezen, a city in the Peloponnese; and in the first act we find an indication that it is day, but that is all. Where setting in time and space is integral in Shakespeare, it has no consequence in Racine. "One thinks," Olson concludes, "of some cold abstract pavilion in eternity; or rather, one does not really think of it at all" (226).

Finally, Shakespeare's characters are, likewise, particularized. The more central of them have individual temperaments, moral principles, thoughts. Ordinarily, we even know something of their histories. Olson illustrates with Hamlet. Among other characteristics, he is a scholar, and Shakespeare has him speak, even in a moment of extreme agitation, in metaphors which liken his thoughts to books:

> Remember thee!
> Yea, from the table of my memory
> I'll wipe away all trivial fond records,
> All saws of books, all forms, all pressures past
> That youth and observation have copied there
> And thy commandment all alone shall live
> Within the book and volume of my brain
> . . . .

> My tables—meet it is I set it down
> That one may smile and smile and be a villain.

We know also many other things about Hamlet. He is interested
in plays and players; he is a soldier; he dresses well; he is
an expert fencer; he loves music and poetry. All this knowledge
affects the way in which he thinks, talks, acts.

Of Phèdre, we know only generally her character, the situation
she is in, and how she feels. Shakespeare's particularization of
character is especially felt at high moments of the plays. A
comparison of Hamlet's soliloquies, with that of Phèdre in Act
IV, Scene V, is revealing. When Hamlet speaks, everything he
is—his likes, his dislikes, his reading, his whole history—has its
use. Of Phèdre, on the contrary, "we see only the movement of
her thought, and her consequent feelings, and all this very
generally" (227).

Olson then lists more ways in which Shakespeare and Racine
differ. Shakespeare successfully uses comic scenes and characters
in his most serious plays because he is concerned with a *succession of events* in which an interlude of the ridiculous can
heighten the terror. His comic scenes, says Olson, "may be comic
in abstraction from the play; they are not in context; who ever
laughed during the porter scene in *Macbeth*, or the gravedigger
scene in *Hamlet?*" (230). Racine, however, so concentrates on
single actions and situations that he must maintain the same
tone throughout or lose it—a thing cannot be tragic and comic
at the same time. Further, there are Shakespeare's elaborate subplots; Racine does not use them at all. Finally, Shakespeare turns
his expositions into stories interesting in their own right (the
ghost story in *Hamlet;* the encounter with the witches in *Macbeth;* the whole first act of *Othello*); Racine gets his expositions
over in a rush and is interested only in essentials.

Shakespeare, Olson says, "studies the whole complex of issues
about a given issue, and that issue is given meaning by its complex relations" (229). In *Lear*, the major issue is self-love versus
love of others; and, in order to exhibit it, Shakespeare shows it
operating in "*all* familial relations (father-daughter, daughter-
father, father-son, son-father, husband-wife, wife-husband, etc.)
all economic relations (master-servant, servant-master) and all

political relations (king-subject, lord-vassal, etc)" (229). Racine, on the other hand, studies only the major issue, in isolation and universally, without qualifying it circumstantially. In a last word on the two opposing methods, Olson notes that Shakespeare *enriches* his material; Racine *refines* his.

Each of the two methods is unique in the way it affects its audience and displays the universal. Olson contends that Racine pares away—with a loss of emotion, though not a complete one—the circumstances and presents the universal as directly as possible. "The universal," Olson continues, "is of course always in Shakespeare, but we have to win our way toward it through circumstance and accident, just as we win our way toward experience and wisdom and science in life" (232). Shakespeare's method seems the more effective, not because the universal, in the sense Olson has just described, is not more affecting than immediate perception, but because what we have earned, and what has truly engaged our feelings, is more vivid and more treasured. For something immediate to sense to "truly" engage our feelings, it must be worthy in a qualitative sense, must involve images, not only vivid ones but ones of *importance*. I hasten to add, however, that "the tragedy of thinking and reasoning," as Olson describes Racine's contribution to the drama, presupposes an audience which has already attained to wisdom and which is capable of understanding that universals are embedded in particulars and of going directly to them.

IV   *T. S. Eliot*

Olson has not written an essay on T. S. Eliot as a lyric poet (which he preeminently is), but he has written about *Murder in the Cathedral* in a way which emphasizes Eliot's lyrical talent. The discussion of *Murder in the Cathedral* opens ironically with a comment on the attractiveness of the medieval costumes which cannot help but recall Aristotle's distinction between the costumer's art and that of the poet. Though Olson, of course, would not deny the title of poet to Eliot, he thinks he has failed in the most central way as a playwright in *Murder in the Cathedral;* the work has no true plot and

cannot, therefore, be a true drama. He has some questions to
ask about the action, especially its central feature, the
martyrdom. Becket's course does not strike him as a "patently" right one. He cannot see why it is a moral necessity for
the Becket of the play (as distinct from the historical figure)
to die; how his death could help the Church; or why he makes
it so easy for the Knights to kill him. Nor will Olson accept
the idea that Eliot, rather than making the action a necessary
or probable one, simply assumes the audience will side with
Christianity and the Church. To Olson, a dramatist has no
business making such assumptions. "It is his business to make
a play that will stand on its own legs. The cheap popular
writer, for the sake of a quick and easy effect, may hook on
to any belief or predisposition of his public, even very ephemeral ones, for these will not be so ephemeral as his work;
but the serious artist must anchor his foundations in human
nature itself" (252).

Further, Olson thinks there must be more to martyrdom and
sainthood than simply deciding to be killed. In *Murder in the
Cathedral* there is no anguish. Olson comments that Eliot
makes sainthood sound easier than becoming a full professor.
Looking at the historical murder of Becket, Olson sees "a
tremendous human drama, pregnant with grave issues, charged
with passion." Looking at Eliot's poem, he finds only a "shal-
low and tepid conception" of the historic event. The characters are no more than "participants in a discourse within his
[Eliot's] mind, not distinct dramatic entities. The Knights
themselves are only Eliot stating his idea ironically" (253).

Yet the poem is one in which a better effect is obtained
when, as Olson notes, it is "recited, with suitable gestures, by
actors in costume" (251). Though there is no true dramatic
action, Eliot creates the illusion there is one. Olson uses
Becket's discussion with his Four Tempters as illustration.
Just as Becket himself is one of the participants in a discussion
within Eliot's mind, so the Four Tempters exist only in Becket's
mind as personifications of four courses of action open to him.
There is, however, no real conflict, no real engagement of feelings; for Becket has rejected three of the courses before they

are presented, and the fourth offers no true obstacle. Unlike the supernatural elements in *Macbeth*, in *Hamlet*, or in *The Tempest* which are explicable within the plays of which they are parts and which are germane to their actions, Eliot presents the Tempters as something within Becket's mind; and yet, without explaining how it is possible, Eliot has Becket tell the women and Priests of Canterbury to watch.

If the poem fails as a play, how can we, asks Olson, account for its power? "The answer," he says, "is as easy as [Eliot's] sainthood. Eliot exerts many and powerful lyric devices to do what he cannot do dramatically . . . The piece is simply an extended lyric poem (a very fine one!) in which the object of the poet's emotion, rather than being the west wind or the skylark, is a kind of story" (254). The best that can be made of *Murder in the Cathedral* in a dramatic sense would be to liken it to the choric spectacles of Phyrnichus who was, we remember, a forerunner of Aeschylus with whom this discussion of drama began.

CHAPTER 6

Practical Criticism: The Shorter Forms

I *Alexander Pope*

OLSON's treatment of Pope is applicable to the greater
part of his work.[2] Olson, who approaches Pope through
the long-standing argument between the romantics and neo-
classicists as to whether Pope really is a "poet," points out that
many of those who defend Pope as a poet[3] do so with the
romantic definitions of poet and poetry held by those who
would deny him the title. In fact, most of the defenses of Pope
evince "rather an ability to find romantic qualities in the
neo-classical than any real ability for the appraisal of the neo-
classical itself" (19). Under Olson's divisions of poetry into
imitative and didactic a small number of Pope's poems, such as
Windsor Forest, might be called *imitative*. A good many more,
however, among them the satires, are didactic and rhetorical.
In either of these cases Pope is entitled, according to Olson's
latest views, to be called poet; but "rhetorician" is perhaps
the most apt word for his chief talents.

Olson thinks that, in pointing to the rhetorical side of Pope,
he is doing what should have been done much sooner; that
most competent writers about Pope have, in fact, treated him
as a rhetorician.

Although Olson proposes, then, to treat Pope on the basis
of rhetorical principles, he makes it plain immediately that by
"rhetoric" he does not mean the "truncated modern" view which
substitutes a part, such as considerations of style, for the whole
apparatus of persuasion. Olso thinks Pope's practice can best
be exemplified from Aristotle's *Rhetoric;* and, to substantiate

his position, he undertakes an analysis of Pope's *Epistle to Dr. Arbuthnot*. Olson prefaces the inquiry into the *Epistle* by pointing out that Aristotle has delineated three modes of persuasion in speech: the character of the speaker (properly drawn, his character makes the audience accept things not demonstrated); the state of mind of the audience; and the contents of the speech.

Before discussing the *Epistle* under these three modes of persuasion, Olson notes, first, Pope's rhetorical acumen in casting his *defense* (the *Epistle*, Olson says, is an example of forensic rhetoric) in the form of a dialogue. By showing himself, closeted with a good friend of such outstanding reputation as Arbuthnot, Pope, in Olson's view, puts himself in a congenial and positive setting. The presence of Arbuthnot serves to "validate . . . both the argument and the report of it which constitute the *Epistle*" (22).

Further, the dialogue device permits Pope to be seemingly unaware of any other auditor than Arbuthnot and to employ all the rhetorical devices while seeming to use none. Second, it is excellent strategy for Pope to cast his answer in the form of a "bill of complaint." This procedure indicates he does not consider the charges against him serious enough to be answered directly, and he shifts the burden of proof to his opponents.

Olson begins the rhetorical analysis with the "character" of the speaker. Aristotle says the speaker's character will be most effective if he shows "good sense, good moral character, and good will." Pope uses "a dozen devices" to characterize himself as a man of good sense: "his attitude toward flatterers (11. 109-24), toward fools (*passim*); toward sober criticism (11. 156-7), toward bad art (11. 33-46), and in general by his sharp insight into character and motive" (23). His characterization of himself as morally good, Olson observes, is even more extensive. At one place or another Pope indicates that he possesses a whole catalogue of virtues: "He is courageous (11. 371-2); temperate (if we can so construe 1. 263); liberal, (11. 368-87), properly ambitious (11. 334 ff.), gentle (11. 368-87), "amicable (11. 35, 37), sincere in self profession" (11. 261 ff.), witty (this scarcely requires illustration), and just" (11. 283 ff.) (23). Pope easily shows himself of good will, because he characterizes the audience as people who, like himself love virtue and hate vice.

What has been said about the speaker's character is sufficient to show that Pope has not omitted many virtues, but we have not displayed the chief technique through which Pope proves himself to possess the characteristics he claims: the dialogue. The dramatized situation allows him to avoid direct statement and simply to show himself acting virtuously. Simulated drama is better than statement that is analytic and subject to examination and refutation, for dramatization presents in a lifelike way a complex of characteristics not easy to pin down. A statement, too, is secondhand and not so convincing as that which is actually seen:

> Notice how the attribution proceeds by dramatization; in lines 333 ff., for example, Pope breaks into a heroic declamation which has the effect of attributing extremest moral excellence to him; he does not, however, *state* that he is virtuous; he merely shows himself as if he were. . . . The moral indignation which he assumes in the angry interruptions (e.g., 11. 78 ff.), the ironic amusement at flattery (e.g., 11. 115 ff.), the regret at the fate of Gay (11. 256 ff.), the apparent justice of the portrait of Atticus, the earnestness of such passages as lines 135 ff., as lines 261 ff., as lines 334 ff.— all these are speeches appropriate only to a man of distinguished virtue and prudence (24-25).

A rhetorical work is ordered by the need to convince an audience—in this case, one of the virtuous. The assumption is that the virtuous have become angry with Pope because of the charges of his accusers, and they fear and hate him. As Olson indicates, Pope's rhetoric in the *Epistle* seems directed at removing all prejudices against himself as a "mad dog" satirist. He must begin, Olson contends, by allaying any fear the reader may have that he is the next to be attacked; to exempt the reader, he shows himself as besieged by such a "rabble of bad poets" that he is unlikely to be able to attack anyone else, and he characterizes his enemies as insane and as, therefore, to be feared rather than himself.

After this initial sally at the opinion of the audience, in the course of which Pope has shown himself to be kind even to servants and mad poets and to have been falsely accused, he proceeds gradually to remove any prejudices which might still be held against him: "The audience may feel that while Pope's satire is certainly not unprovoked, the punishment may be excessive, and Pope, consequently, may be cruel. This charge is answered in lines 83-101, and it is notable that Pope himself raises the question rather than Arbuthnot: as one who punishes justly, Pope must himself have weighed the punishment" (27).

Pope continues to work at allaying the prejudices of the audience until line 124; thereafter, he tries to make the audience view him positively through the catalogue of great ones who have approved his work; though the appeal to the pity of the audience ("The Muse but serv'd to ease some friend, not Wife, / To help me thro' this long disease, my life" [11. 131-3]), and through the earlier appeal based on his natural ability to write ("As yet a child, nor yet a fool to fame, / I lisp'd in numbers, for the numbers came" [11. 127-8]). When Pope feels that the audience has been persuaded, he proceeds with restraint to attack Gildon and Dennis; for the audience is not so definitely his that he can attack with full power. A momentary flurry of vituperation at the "more sober" critics is, at once, intensified and tempered by the metaphor in lines 167-72:

> Ev'n such small critics some regard may claim,
> Preserv'd in *Milton's* or in *Shakespeare's* name.
> Pretty! in amber to observe the forms
> Of hairs, or straws, or dirt, or grubs, or worms!
> The things we know are neither rich nor rare,
> But wonder how the devil they got there.

After more restrained attack comes the portrait of Atticus when the audience is more under control but when Pope still doesn't feel completely free to release all his fire. The placement of the portrait is perfect, for Pope wouldn't want to be too direct with Addison under any circumstances: he is too well esteemed; besides, he is not the principal foe. The portrait of Atticus is too famous to require much comment; but, as Olson notes, "Pope, using what Aristotle calls 'a method of thoroughly skillful and unscrupulous prosecutors,' mixes the virtues and vices of Atticus in such a fashion as to disguise perfectly that this is special pleading" (28).

Pope, still cautious about his audience, follows the portrait with a long passage (11. 215-70) in which he attempts to show he has not attacked Addison because of literary envy; there are poets, like *Bufo,* who seek patrons, but Pope is not one of them. This conciliatory passage is followed by additional characterization which states that Pope never intentionally gave offense in his work and that some works attributed to him are not his: "Poor guiltless I! and can I choose but smile, / When ev'ry Coxcomb knows me by my *Style?*" (11. 281-82). Then, with the situation at its best so far as audience control is concerned, Pope fires his heaviest weapons against Sporus. Sporus is perhaps no "butterfly" as Arbuthnot suggests; be that as it may, the "painted child of dirt, that stinks and stings" is broken on the wheel of Pope's polemic, and his most prominent features are what suffer most disfiguration. The smashing of Sporus removes all charges against Pope, and he ends the poem by touching up the virtuous portrait of himself that he has all along been painting.

The third rhetorical device, the argument of the piece, has three parts which correspond to Pope's progress in winning the audience and what he does when that aim is accomplished. To Olson, the argument is relatively simple: the first part (11. 1-124) argues that Pope's present action is justifiable; the second (11. 125-248), that Pope did not begin the literary war in which he is engaged; the third (11. 49-end) begins with Pope's guarantee of his future conduct and ends with the final destruction of his enemies and with the final establishment of his character.

Olson, who considers diction last, is convinced that "the style, the prosody, and even the grammatical constructions are appropriate" (31). First, the style is in the tradition of the great rhetoricians, Horace, Juvenal, and Persius; to write thus is to invoke their authority. Second, the diction is appropriate because it is tailored to exhibit character, evoke the desired emotions, and suit the subject matter. Olson illustrates with the passage where Pope describes the simplicity of his outlook on life:

> Oh let me live my own, and die so too!
> (To live and die is all I have to do)
> Maintain a Poet's dignity and ease,
> And see what friends, and read what books I please:
> Above a Patron, tho' I condescend
> Sometimes to call a Minister my friend.
> I was not born for Courts or great affairs;
> I pay my debts, believe, and say my pray'rs;
> Can sleep without a Poem in my head,
> Nor know if *Dennis* be alive or dead. (11. 261-70)

The passage employs, in their literal sense, simple words, most of them monosyllables; and its grammar is straightforward and unambiguous. Such a diction, as Olson oberves, makes for clarity; but, to understand how appropriate it is to the character, feeling, and subject, all we have to do is imagine how an elaborate diction would have failed. More specifically, Olson thinks the subjunctive structure ("Oh let me live my own, etc.") sets an emotional tone which couldn't have been achieved with a declarative sentence ("I wish to live my own") and that such a feeling is proper because "the good man ought not merely to wish a good life but to feel strongly about it, so that all his emotions are ordered to it; and the best argument that one has such and such desires is the exhibition of one's self as actually moved by the contemplation of them" (31). On the other hand, to have repeated the "Oh let me" at the beginning of each line would have made the whole speech border on the hysterical. The briefness of the passage too is proper. It would not do to make a detailed statement about the "simple" life. Finally, though the diction is plain it is "saved from meanness through its employment in moral discourse, through the absence of any low referents, and through the verse" (32).

Olson concludes his view of Pope with some remarks about the form of the poem. He points out that, though the rhetoric is circular, "the warrant for credibility of the argument is the character of Pope, and, strangely enough, the particular arguments establishing each trait of character depend upon the previous assumption that Pope has the very trait in question" (32). This circularity is not ruinous, Olson contends, because

"Pope's lively simulation of virtue, . . . is sufficiently impressive to establish part, and hence all, of the circle" (33).

In Olson's view, the criticism of Pope has tended to dwell on the limitations imposed on him by the conventions within which he was working. One of the chief merits of Olson's methods is its aim to discover what the works of Pope are, not what they are not.

II *William Butler Yeats*

Olson's essay on Yeats is of interest because of its general relevance to Yeats's poetry: because of its particular analysis of "Sailing to Byzantium"; and because of what that analysis provides as a critical exemplum. Olson is essentially concerned with the principal part of "Sailing to Byzantium," the activity imitated in the poem. As it turns out, the poem's activity is cast as an argument. Olson, therefore, states that argument and shows how the logical necessities of the poem's dialectic equate with the probabilities which tie events together in other kinds of imitative poems.

Olson clearly modified his view of this particular poem in the six-year interval between the essay here considered, "Sailing to Byzantium: Prolegomena to a Poetics of the Lyric" (1942),[4] and *An Outline of Poetic Theory* (1948). The modifiication involves his recognition that the "argument" *is* the "activity" of the poem and that, consequently, the character of its speaker is determined by that action rather than, as he stated in the earlier essay, "by its role in a drama, not of action, but of thought" (219). This modification is important, because the unwarranted distinction between "thought" and "activity" has been eliminated. As Olson has observed more recently: "Are not incidents in the soul as much incidents as fist-fights and horse-races? Is the 'secret inner life' not activity? If not, what is it?"[5]

Before proceeding to analyze the "action" of the poem, Olson paraphrases its contents:

In "Sailing to Byzantium" an old man faces the problem of old age, of death, and of regeneration, and gives his decision. Old age, he tell us, excludes a man from the sensual joys of youth; the world appears to belong completely to the young; . . . indeed an old man is scarcely a man at all—he is an empty artifice; . . . he is a tattered coat upon a stick. This would be very bad, except that the young are also excluded from something; rapt in their sensuality, they are ignorant utterly of the world of the spirit. Hence if old age frees a man from sensual passion, he may rejoice in the liberation of the soul; he is admitted into the realm of the spirit; and his rejoicing will increase according as he realizes the magnificence of the soul. But the soul can best learn its own greatness from the great works of art; . . . in turning to them he finds that these are by no means mere effigies, or monuments, but things which have souls also; . . . hence he prays for death, for release from his mortal body; and . . . he wishes reincarnation, not now in a mortal body, but in the immortal and changeless embodiment of art. (211-12)

The terms around which the poem is organized are a series of oppositions—youth, sensually active but spiritually passive; the kind of old age which lacks both sensuality and spirituality; old age which has spiritual capacity though it is physically incapacitated; art considered as inanimate (as "monuments"); and art as animate (artificial birds with human souls).

With the content of the poem stated, the analysis of the argument, the "activity," begins. In the first two stanzas (the first half of the poem), art is considered as inanimate and, in the second two, as animate. In the first two stanzas, the "images of Byzantium" are considered as objects of contemplation; in the second two, they are treated as gods who can consume the last shred of the old man's sensuality; consume his heart (the symbol of all that is opposed to pure intellect); and make him, like themselves, insouled in the incorruptible.

Olson points to still other divisions within the two halves of the poem. Stanza one demonstrates that youth occupies itself only with "Whatever is begotten, born, and dies"—with the transient and the corruptible. This way of life is not satisfactory; passion, and the sensuality which underlies it, must be rejected. Stanza two begins with the rejection of mere old age; it is worse than youth, for it does not even have passion. As the stanza progresses, however, the old man finds that, as he con-

templates the soul's monuments, the arts, his soul develops
even as his body decays, and that the resulting gain in intellect
is more than a substitute for the lost passion of youth. In
stanza three, the great discovery is made that the "monuments"
contain souls, and the old man realizes that the body in which
his soul resides is not only dying but that physical appetites
and passion always have trammeled the spiritual. He understands that the death of his body is a prerequisite for the recon-
ciliation he seeks. In stanza four, he sees the possibility of an
incorruptible residence for his soul in such beautiful artifices as
the golden birds of Byzantium; and he says he will seek such
a place for his soul. Let me add that, though the thought of
the soul reincarnated in a work of art is a beautiful and extremely moving particularization, even monuments disappear
in time; and the major recognition of the poem is that the soul,
finally, is its own place.

Olson points to additional structural values of the poem
which are both organic and geometric. In stanza one, a living
bird among true trees sings in praise of mortality; in stanza
four, however, "an immortal and artificial bird set in an artificial tree sings an eternal song of spiritual joy in praise of
eternal things" (213). The song of mortality—"whatever is begotten, born, and dies"—is perfectly paralleled with the song of
immortality: "what is past, or passing or to come." In stanza
two, a living being, an old man without spirituality, is found
to be an inanimate thing—"A tattered coat upon a stick"; but,
in stanza three, the apparently inanimate monuments of art
are found to possess souls. Furthermore, says Olson, "A certain
artificial symmetry in the argument serves to distinguish these
parts even further: stanzas I and IV begin with the conclusions
of their respective arguments, whereas II and III end with
their proper conclusions, and I is dependent upon II for the
substantiation of its premises, as four is dependent upon III"
(213).

In discussing how the argument just outlined functions as
the soul of the poem, as its "plot," Olson rejects theories of
poetry that depend on the chance associations of the reader
with certain words or on the dictionary meanings of the terms
used in a poem. Rather, he says, as he has said many times,

the terms in poetry take their meanings from context. He illustrates the point with a reference to the way in which the ordinary meaning of the word "singing" is extended in "Sailing to Byzantium." In the poem "singing" means both the "rejoicing of the natural creature and that of the artificial; as a consequence, all the terms which relate to jubilation and song are affected; for example, 'commend,' 'music,' 'singing-school,' and 'singing masters' suffer an extension commensurate with that of singing'" (216). He continues by observing that a similar extension happens to the term "intellect" and all related terms; that the word "monuments" is used to mean not ordinary monuments but "changeless embodiments of the changeless soul." Byzantium is not a historical city—"the tourist is not invited to recall that here once he was overcharged, nor is the historian invited to contribute such information as that this was a city visited by Hugh of Vermandois" (216).

Seeing that Olson's later thought tends to be inconsistent with some of the things he has said here about the argument of the poem as its principle, let me attempt briefly a reconstruction. The "choice" made in the poem is for the morally preferable condition in which the soul is dominant. The speaker in the poem, whose character is exhibited by the choice he makes and by his capacity for making it the way he does, reaches his choice by means of the poem's argument. The "plot" then, instead of consisting of a series of incidents, is the various phases of the argument which is held together, not by ordinary probability and possibility, but by dialectical relationships. It is an "activity" of a *definite moral quality* undertaken by an appropriate character.

III *Wallace Stevens*[6]

Elder Olson argues that to consider Wallace Stevens a philosopher, as many have, is to do both him and philosophy a disservice. A philosopher is concerned with constructing a universe of discourse in which he can advance arguments relating to man and his world and even about literary theory. The philosopher's primary concern is with ideas. The poet, too, is concerned with ideas, but thoughts are not so primarily his aim as are the particulars in which they can be embodied. All thought, says Olson again, involves the framing of images and, as a consequence, the entertainment of ideas; but, depending on whether the chief concern is thought or feeling, the emphasis is on idea or image:

> In science the image exists for the sake of the idea, and is unimportant except as it conveys or fails to convey the idea; in poetry the case is opposite. For example, if you think the idea *triangle,* you make a mental picture of it; if your concern is intellectual, it does not matter what sort of triangle you picture, red or blue, small or large, right, scalene, or equilateral, for you disregard the special character of the image and go on with the idea. But if your concern is with ideas in their emotional aspect, the image is more important than the idea, for what we actually imagine affects us more powerfully than something we merely conceive. (395-96)

This argument is essentially the one Olson consistently advances to support such conceptions as his view of the ethical effects of imitative poetry; his theory of the emotions; the basic difference between Racine and Shakespeare; and, his assessment of the value of dramatic manner and its counterpart in lyric poetry, imagery. What Olson has said is patently correct; but he should have made more explicit an important implication of his view: that the quality of the situation or image which poetry presents is of supreme importance since only those images which are greatly conceived are capable of seriously moving an audience. It makes a good deal of difference, for example, whether death is presented in the sentimental imagery of the "graveyard school," the exaggeration of which makes it impossible to entertain seriously, or whether, as in Emily Dickinson's "I Heard a Fly Buzz When I Died" or Wallace Stevens' "The Emperor of Ice-Cream," the images present a view of death which is both important and inescapably plausible.

We have been discussing images in more than one sense; in the largest sense, we mean the complex of images which results from everything the poet presents—either directly as on the stage, or through various narrative devices in the lyric and in the novel—and which provides the particulars from which we

extract universals. In a smaller though corollary sense we mean
the element of narrative technique which a poet employs to
lend as vivid an approximation as he can of a direct sensation.
Olson thinks Wallace Stevens can most profitably be considered
as a poet whose chief strength is his skill with imagery in
this sense.

To illustrate this view, Olson analyzes two of Stevens' poems,
the first of which is "Life is Motion":

> In Oklahoma
> Bonnie and Josie
> Dressed in Calico
> Danced around a stump.
> They cried,
> "Ohoyaho,
> Ohoo,"
> Celebrating the marriage
> of flesh and air.

Olson says that, if we consider the image which we see when
we read this poem, the first thing which strikes us is that it
is more complete than the poem: "We imagine two little girls,
in an ecstasy of joy; they wear quaint, stiff, 'dutchy' dresses
made out of calico flour sacking; they cry out shrilly as they
dance with clumsy abandon around a stump, against a background of farm land" (396).

We could not prove all this detail from the poem—there is
no direct reference to the age of the girls, to farm life, or to
the degree of grace or lack of it with which they dance. As
Olson puts it on the vexing matter of what we can read into
a poem, "We ought not to read anything and everything into
poetry; but also we ought not to concentrate on the bare words
of a poem and leave out what the human intellect, imagination, and emotion are likely to make of them" (396-97). Then
Olson asks us to look at the poem with him, to find that the
first two lines are without images but contain elements which
could affect images. The third line, joined with the first two,
produces the image of two little girls in calico: "two little
girls are suggested by feminine diminutive names . . . and
Oklahoma' now joins with 'calico' to suggest home-made dresses

of print flour sacking" (397). The fourth line puts the girls in joyful motion. The line's rhythm suggests their clumsiness (try, Olson says, substituting "round" for "around," and the suggestion is for a more graceful motion than the hopping quality which "around" suggests), while the stump (together with the earlier "calico") suggests a farm background rather than either a city or oil field both of which Oklahoma also contains. The fifth line simply says the girls cried out, and the sixth and seventh lines actually render their exuberant cries of joy.

The last two lines afford an insight into the cause of the girl's dance. We must interpret the metaphor, "the marriage of flesh and air." When we do, we realize that the "celebration" is caused by the basic relationship between the motion of the dance and that which underlies all life. The conclusion, the idea that life is motion, comes with force because we have, in a sense, experienced the fact of it along with Bonnie and Josie.

Olson engages in a similar exercise on "The Emperor of Ice-Cream":

> Call the roller of big cigars,
> The muscular one, and bid him whip
> In kitchen cups concupiscent curds.
> Let the wenches dawdle in such dress
> As they are used to wear, and let the boys
> Bring flowers in last month's newspapers.
> Let be be finale of seem.
> The only emperor is the emperor of ice-cream.
>
> Take from the dresser of deal,
> Lacking the three glass knobs, that sheet
> On which she embroidered fantails once
> And spread it so as to cover her face.
> If her horny feet protude, they come
> To say how cold she is, and dumb.
> Let the lamp affix its beam.
> The only emperor is the emperor of ice-cream.

This poem differs from "Life is Motion" in which the sight and sounds of the two little girls cause the speaker (or poet) to achieve an insight; for in "The Emperor" the series of images illustrates a prior state of mind. "He says what he says," in Olson's words, "because he feels revulsion at the conventional notion of the dignity of death, the old idea that Death is the king of kings, the only true emperor" (398). The poem's speaker has decided this idea is not true: death is not king; no one who is alive really sees any dignity in it. The cynical orders the speaker gives in stanza one (each of them in contravention of some funereal custom) show that the wake in which the living participate (in such a vulgar fashion) is much more important to them than the funeral. We do not even really know that it is a funeral preparation or that the normal funeral fare has been replaced with "concupiscent curds" until the fourth line of stanza two. In stanza two, we find that the dead woman is not only undignified in death (covered with an embroidered sheet), but old (horny feet) and also poor (the cheap dresser with missing knobs). The unimportance of death to the living is underlined: all the sight of her dead feet can do is show how little she has to do with life.

These poems, to Olson, are typical Stevens performances, and Olson is now ready to be more general. The first point he makes is that the little girls and the dead old woman are not really present in the poems as characters but as objects of someone's thought even though they are in "center stage"; and all we know of his thought and feeling must be drawn from what he says about them. The "someone" of Stevens' poems is always the same character ("however fantastically disguised"); but, although Olson doesn't directly say so, the kind of man he is—one capable of such subtleties of thought, feeling, and expression—augments the effects of the poems.

Olson cannot find a Stevens poem which involves "an exciting external situation, or the drama of a tremendous moral choice, or violent and immediate passion" (398). He finds him always aloof, always an observer, of the feelings of others and sometimes even of his own. Stevens tends, Olson thinks, to view men collectively rather than individually; he is a spectator of life, the connoisseur of, rather than participant in, the "fundamental ecstasy and anguish of the human soul" (398).

The Stevens of the poems confines himself to mental activities,

Olson observes, but they are not strictly rational activities, nor are they philosophic in the sense that Lucretius, who presents a logical argument, is. Olson would prefer to call Stevens' poetic action "a dialectic of the imagination, playing perpetually on the diverse relations of things, ideas, images, and emotions" (399). Stevens sometimes takes an object or an idea and relates it to a series of images, each one productive of a facet of emotion; or he sometimes reverses the procedure and keeps a constant mood or image which he relates to different ideas and objects. To Olson, for this reason many of Stevens' poems approach various musical forms: theme with variations, "13 Ways of Looking at a Blackbird," "Nuances on a Theme by Williams," "Sea Surface Full of Clouds," and "Variations on a Summer Day," or the fugue, "The Pure Good of Theory" and "Description Without Place." Stevens does have what could be considered philosophic materials ("his problems of whether the knower is ever identical with the known, whether the world is the same for all or different for each, whether language can express reality or extend sensation, and so on" [399]); but Olson thinks they are only a single element in his poems. More important, Olson contends, is his kaleidoscopic imagination and the play of images it produces which gives conveyance to his thought and feeling.

What Stevens' work lacks in human drama, it makes up for with its imagery. Images, Olson reiterates, appeal to the senses almost as a painting does. This visual imagery dominates Stevens' work, and, to Olson, he has a rare talent for seeing things as a painter does. To illustrate, Olson lists titles which suggest, this time, pictures: "Bantams in Pine Woods," "Landscape with Boat." "He can," Olson continues, "refer to Corot for an autumn evening, to Franz Hals for a cloudscape. One almost looks for the signature of Cezanne under 'Study of Two Pears,' of Renoir under 'Poems of Our Time'" (400). He is even successful, Olson muses, with that sure way to "poetic shipwreck": the catalogue of colors. Olson's examples need to be quoted:

He knows how to heighten colors and set them against a contrasting background, as in "rouged fruits in early snow";

how to modify them sharply and effectively, as in "blunt
yellow," "dense violet"; even how to suggest them without
mentioning them (note how many colors spring to mind in
"The Emperor of Ice-Cream," though none is mentioned). He
knows the importance of light and shade ("The shadows of
the pears / Are blobs on the green cloth") and the influence
of atmosphere on objects (observe how bright the tigers are
in "tigers in red weather"). And he can draw upon a palette
whose colors range from the stark, gaudy flatness of circus
posters to such luminous transparencies as "the dove with
eye of grenadine" and "Triton dissolved in shifting diaphanes
/ Of blue and green. . . ." (401)

Marvelous as these visual images are in themselves, Olson
thinks their full effect can be realized only if their relationship to ideas and feelings is fully understood. To elaborate, he
proposes that everyone, through habit or convention, connects
certain ideas with certain systems of imagery and certain emotions with certain objects. Such connections, Olson thinks,
vary from people to people and have "profound roots in the
whole character of a society, because they involve beliefs and
attitudes which concern what is true or false, good or bad,
beautiful or ugly" (401). Olson likens the situation to a switch-
board which the artist can use, and depend on, just as it is—
or whose connections he can change. It should already be clear
that in such a poem as "The Emperor of Ice-Cream" Stevens
violates the conventions concerning death by exposing their
hypocrisy and, by implication, his own genuine concern.

"More than anything," Olson continues, "it is the collapse
of belief in our day—beliefs religious, ethical, political, metaphysical, even aesthetic—which moves him" (401). As in the
case of "The Emperor of Ice-Cream," Stevens satirizes the
false, but he is also concerned with the truth. In the search
for values, says Olson, Stevens has conceived the "notion of
poetry as the supreme fiction constructed to replace belief, and
of the imagination as the architect of that fiction" (401-402).
Olson thinks that Stevens, no longer able to believe in the
things once thought heroic and divine, but, still convinced of
the reality of the heroic and divine, sought to invent better
things to which to ascribe them.

Olson concludes by warning the reader not to expect a logical structure in poems controlled by images; imagistic poems have simply to be contemplated and felt. Olson thinks Stevens "has one of the most exquisitely fastidious minds of our age," and that "any contact whatsoever with it, perfect or imperfect, is certain to be exciting and valuable" (402).

IV *Marianne Moore*

Olson's brief article on Marianne Moore[7] establishes with accuracy the essence of her verse. He contends that Miss Moore is not in the mainstream of modern poetry. He believes that, in spite of T. E. Hulme's 1913 prediction that a classical age in poetry was imminent, most modern poetry is basically romantic; that, however T. S. Eliot might protest, he, for example, bears a closer resemblance to Keats, Shelley, and Tennyson than he does to Dryden or to Pope. On the other hand, Olson thinks Miss Moore is in a "classical" tradition which stems from the *Satires* and *Epistles* of Horace.

When a critic contrasts the terms "romantic" and classical," one or the other of them is usually treated pejoratively; but Olson treats both positively. The "romantic," to him, includes all the great poetic forms and the larger part of all poetry. What he says is, I think, important for its theoretical content as well as for its relevance to Marianne Moore:

> The greater part of poetry, whether narrative, dramatic, or lyric, depends upon what might be called the principle of the extraordinary. The poet invents some action which involves an extraordinary crisis, serious or comic, in human affairs, or invents extraordinary characters, or deals with the human soul in extraordinary states of passion, imagination, intellection, or perception. The extraordinary is selected to begin with, or techniques of amplification or depreciation are used to make something extraordinary. Tragedy and comedy, epic and mock-epic, almost all forms of lyric, depend upon this principle. (100-101)

In contrast to poetry based on the "principle of the extraordinary," there is a poetry which deals "with ordinary matters and normal mental conditions" (101). Such poetry, Olson continues, can employ images; but when it does, it presents direct sensations unmodified by either feeling or imagination. This poetry is intellectual in character, but its intellectual aspect is never made to seem profound. What profundities it may contain are presented matter-of-factly or, as Olson describes it, "as a kind of sublimated common sense." Poetry of this type avoids obvious art and models itself on ordinary discourse, on "personal discussion."

Miss Moore's poetry is of the type just described because it depends, in part, on "personal discussion"; and the kind of person who presents the discussion is important to the effect of the poetry. Miss Moore does not, in the fashion of Yeats or Browning, create various speakers for various poems; but, rather like Stevens, she uses in all of them a single character, ostensibly herself. In spite of singleness of characterization, Miss Moore achieves variety by causing her mind to play over many objects. Though the character which emerges from the poems is never obtrusive—Olson says Miss Moore realizes that, if poetry is to be something like conversation, it ought not to be concerned mainly with herself—she is nevertheless quite easy to describe: "She is honest, just, prudent, shrewd, urbane, witty, fastidious, courageous, and a great deal beside; we know her to be so, not because she makes any attempt to convince us, but because the feelings and opinions to which she gives voice, and the manner in which she voices them, could only have origin in one of that nature" (101). In addition to these virtues, and most importantly, Miss Moore exhibits a quality of mind which Olson confesses is difficult to describe. "Perhaps," he says, "one might call it an imagination with more precision than sensation because it is governed by an intellect more precise than either" (101-102); and Olson states that he means that she deals with great force with what he calls "the fact perfectly known," which, to him, is the "hardest of all things to imagine" (102). He proceeds to illustrate with some of Miss Moore's images: first, a porcupine—"as when the lightning shines / on thistlefine spears, among / prongs in lanes above lanes of a shorter prong . . ."; the racehorse, Tom Fool—

You've the beat
of a dancer to a measure or harmonious rush
    of a porpoise at the prow where the racers
    all win easily—
like centaurs' legs in tune, as when kettledrums
compete;
        nose rigid and suede nostrils spread . . . ;

and, finally, a dancer—

    . . . Entranced, were you not, by Solidad?
black-clad solitude that is not sad;
                    like a letter from
Casals; or perhaps say literal alphabet-
    S soundholes in a 'cello
set contradictorily; or should we call her

la lagarta? or bamboos with fireflies a-glitter;
or glassy lake and the whorls which a vertical
                    stroke brought about
of the paddle half-turned coming out.
    As if bisecting
a viper, she can dart down three times and
    recover without a disaster, having
been a bull-fighter . . .

Olson points out that these images contain comparisons of a
difficult order, though not the same difficulty as that occasioned by metaphysical conceits whose resemblances must always
be argued. Rather, all her comparisons involve two objects,
both of which are seen "sharply and clearly . . . as by a rare
eye" (102). The resemblance between them is such as only
would be seen by an unusual mind; but, unlike analogy in a
John Donne metaphor, when the resemblance is pointed out,
it is clear and substantial. Olson asserts: "And these are no
fictions, but facts; facts, however, fully and more perfectly
revealed. It would seem on first sight, that nothing could be
deader than facts about ordinary things; to see the dead fact
brought alive in this fashion is to witness something as aston-
ishing and miraculous as the blossoming of Tannhauser's staff"
(102-103).

Olson says of the tone and structure of Miss Moore's poems that, though she is never in a highly emotional situation, she implies a capacity for deep feelings, and that, though her poems are intellectual, she does not proceed by deduction but rather by a species of induction: "an association of insights which culminate almost invariably in a final insight" (103). He illustrates this last point about insight with the opening lines of "Tom Fool at Jamaica":

> Look at Jonah embarking from Joppa,
> deterred by the whale; hard going for a
> statesman whom nothing could detain,
> although one who would not rather die than
> repent.

> Be infallible at your peril, for your
> system will fail, and select as a model the
> schoolboy in Spain
> who at the age of six, portrayed a mule
> and jockey who had pulled up for a snail.

> "There is submerged magnificence, as Victor
> Hugo said." *Sentir avec ardeur;* that's it;
> magnetized by feeling.
> Tom Fool "makes an effort and makes it oftener
> than the rest" . . .

Olson describes the poem as "a little essay on what makes the champion" (103). To seek "infallibility" is not the way to become a champion—Jonah and the schoolboy's drawing are evidence that the unforeseen and the unlikely do happen. The quality which makes a champion lies in "submerged magnificence"—that something which makes the horse respond when response is most needed. Olson contends that we have been made to "see" this quality because we have had to contemplate "Jonah, the jockey, and 'submerged magnificence' " (103). While Jonah may be perfectly familiar to us, he is not so as an example of what the unforseen can do; the jockey pulling up for a snail could, Olson continues, be interpreted variously. But, unless the drawing in the poem serves the function of illustrating the incredible and the opposite of "submerged magnificence" (a champion doesn't give way), it cannot be understood.

Miss Moore is a difficult poet because she demands that her readers read with great care. If the reader misses one point, says Olson, he certainly will miss what follows. Her sense of artistic economy is so highly developed that everything she includes must be understood or everything is lost.

CHAPTER 7

Practical Criticism: Dylan Thomas

NO book of Elder Olson's is better known or has received more praise than *The Poetry of Dylan Thomas*.[1] Published soon after the death of Thomas as the first comprehensive treatment of him, it attracted, and has continued to do so, a good deal of attention. It was given the Poetry Society Award for the best book of poetic criticism for 1954; and the reviewers were, for the most part, very generous. The reliability of reviewers is, without doubt, a matter open to discussion. Even in a case, like this one, with predominantly favorable reviews, it is interesting to note how often a reviewer reveals either his own bias or how little he knows about the book he is reviewing or its author.

Ralph N. Maud of Leeds University, reviewing in *Western Humanities Review*,[2] refuses to be convinced by *any* of Olson's analyses of the poems because he had not, I think, checked his impressions against the poems. His tone is almost one of fright. Watching Elder Olson work with a poet is, to a practicing critic, a chastening experience that is apt to put an insecure one on the defensive. Nicholas Joost writing in *Commonweal*[3] praises the book as the first practical demonstration of the powers of the method of the "Chicago Critics" on "fresh creative work." As a matter of fact, several of Olson's essays on modern poets preceded this book; besides, Mr. Joost doesn't exhibit the least idea of the "Chicago method." Richard Eberhart in *Virginia Quarterly Review*[4] speaks well of Olson's work, but he disagrees with him on his choice of Thomas's most valuable poems on the grounds (not explicit, but definitely implied) that he, as a poet, is a better judge of such matters than Olson who is *only* a scholar. His own scholarship did not include Olson the poet. Finally, there is a fine irony in Dudley Fitt's *Saturday Review*[5] piece. He does know Olson as a poet but he praises him by comparing him to William Empson, for whose critical theories Olson has a monumental distaste. So much for the reviewers.[6]

As is usual with Olson, the approach in *Dylan Thomas* is theoretical, not so much in a general sense, as in a particular one since it proposes a theory of Thomas' art. Thomas' poems, both in general and in specific cases, are treated as illustrations of that theory. The book leaves the reader with many instruments with which to study Thomas and with several excellent examples of the best way to use them. Olson's words about the paraphrases the book includes are applicable to its overall effect: "This book contains a number of paraphrases, for various reasons; but they should in no case be taken as terminating the process of reading the poems; they are merely beginnings. I don't want to give the reader crutches; I want to give him a push" (54). The book does not terminate the study of Thomas, but does provide a generous "push" in the direction of one of the most difficult and rewarding poets of the twentieth century.

I   *The Early Poems*

Olson sees a progression in the work of Thomas from an early, very dark outlook toward one in which he achieved "some portion of light" (20). Whereas the early poems were full of "swarming horrors out of Hieronymous Bosch," the middle ones are "charged with powerful and poignant feelings for others"; and Thomas' later poems, though not a *paradiso*, contain "in the charming natural world of Wales, something of a fore-token of Heaven."

The description of the dark "Universe of the Early Poems" is prefaced with much of Olson's theory of symbolism, which involves the transference of the concept of one thing to that of another, and which, unlike metaphor, does not depend upon likeness. Olson illustrates with a line from the sonnet "Altarwise by owl-light": "The atlas-eater with a jaw for news." Thomas, himself, gives "world-devouring" as a paraphrase for "atlas-eater." Olson says that, in order to know what the line means, a reader must *know* that Thomas has substituted the idea of the atlas, which is only a cartographic representation of the world, for the idea of the world itself. We are not dealing with metaphor, then, but with symbol; for, as Olson observes, "An atlas of maps does not much *resemble* the world. A person unacquainted with maps would be quite baffled by one, I think, until he had some instruction in the conventions of cartography" (4).

The rationale for Olson's discussion of symbolism is the extensive use Thomas makes of symbols, especially in this early period. In order to conjecture the "why" of Thomas' use of symbols, Olson shows why symbols are an effective device of depiction. First, he argues, because symbolism involves the substitution of ideas, it "can cause us to entertain ideas remote from, or totally outside of, ordinary experience, by the extension of ideas we already possess" (10). Second, the symbol—that idea which stands for another—is usually presented as an image; hence, by its direct appeal to the senses, it "can make immediate and vivid what otherwise would be remote and faint, and thus act powerfully upon our thoughts and emotions" (10).

Third, a symbol can focus on a "single aspect of something or cause us to conceive that thing in many aspects simultaneously, and so determine our emotional reactions to it" (10). It makes a good deal of difference, for example, if death is symbolized by a "smiling shadowy angel" or by the corpse "amid all the terrors of the charnel house." Fourth, we can often infer from a symbol something of the "character, beliefs, state of mind, or situation of the person who employed the symbol . . . and a writer can utilize our tendency to make inferences of this kind, depicting the mood, thought, and character of his personages by letting us see the symbolic processes of their minds" (11). In summary, Olson does not deny that metaphor has some of the same powers that he has ascribed to symbol; but he doesn't believe metaphor to be as effective because it represents things as a "manner of speaking." "A symbol, on the contrary, exhibits something to us as an actuality, and so affects us more strongly" (11).

There are, then, natural advantages in symbolism; but the questions remain as to why Thomas uses symbols in such obscure and unusual ways. To Olson, the answer lies in the quality of his imagination. Thomas has been praised for dealing with such "major themes" as "birth, life, love, and death"; but there is, however, nothing in these themes which demand symbolic treatment and the history of literature demonstrates that it is possible to write very bad poetry about them. When Thomas conceives of these themes, he does so with an imagination at once powerful and strange: "His imagination permits him to enter into areas of experience previously unexplored or to unveil new aspects of perfectly common experiences . . . like certain mystics he is often forced into symbol and metaphor simply because there is no familiar way of expressing something in itself so unfamiliar" (12).

Olson then emphasizes this last point about the unfamiliar with an analysis of Thomas' strange imagination:

He sees things quite differently from the way in which we should. We should see flowers on a grave; he sees the dead "who periscope through flowers to the sky." We should see the towering flames after a fire raid; he sees "the fire-dwarfed street." He looks into what we should find opaque, looks down at something we are wont to look up at, looks up where we should look down, peers in where we should peer out, and out where we should look in. (12)

If Thomas is compelled by the eccentric quality of his imaginative vision into the use of symbol, it is relevant to investigate the kinds of symbols he employs. Olson finds three general categories of symbols in Thomas' poems which are determined by their sources: (1) natural, (2) conventional, and (3) private. The first category comprises common symbols everyone is apt to employ: "Light is a symbol of good or knowledge, dark of evil or ignorance, warmth of life or comfort, cold of death or discomfort, ascent of progress or resurrection, descent of regression or death, and so on" (7). Olson cautions against assuming that Thomas never varies the meanings of these symbols, or that they are always symbols: "Surely," he argues, "there are such things as light, dark, warmth, cold, ascent, and descent" (8).

Conventional symbols are more difficult because they require a knowledge of the conventions on which they are based. Thomas draws such symbols from "cartography, astronomy, physics, chemistry, botany, anatomy, mechanics, and in particular such pseudo-sciences as . . . astrology, alchemy, witchcraft . . . from games and sports; from a mass of myth and legend, including some rather recondite rabbinical materials" (8). Olson gives one excellent example of this kind of symbolism when he asks, "What is the meaning of this phrase: 'The twelve triangles of the cherub wind?'" It does no good to approach the phrase, he insists, with any preconceived symbologies. If on the other hand, one will "simply think[,] about winds a bit . . . [he] will be likely to remember the tradition of twelve winds blowing from twelve points of the compass and to recall that ancient maps conventionally represented winds as issuing from a small human head with its puffed-out cheeks blowing furiously" (7).

The private symbolism, Olson thinks, can best be understood by following Thomas from poem to poem. For example, Olson finds him using "wax" as a symbol for flesh, "oil" for life, "scissors" to symbolize both birth and death (the umbilical cord is cut; the thread of life is cut); and many others. Thomas uses all three kinds of symbols to make "immediate and factual" the conceptions of his extraordinary imagination. Although we noted earlier that the world of Thomas' early poems was a dark one, a few words on its shape are in order. Thomas' world is dominated by suffering and death in their most frightening forms. It contains a giant runner in the form of a grave who overtakes everyone; and it is where "cadaver, the one corpse hidden in all flesh . . . wears living men as his masks," and where there is nothing but "darkness and gloom, lit only occasionally by dying planets, baleful eyes or the phosphorescent corruption of the tomb" (15-16).

Though the universe of Thomas' early work is a terrible one, it is not, Olson maintains, a "Grand Guignol" universe. The terror in Thomas is never presented for its own sake, as it is in melodramas which "exaggerate and readily depart from

truth in order to achieve sensation . . . The world of the
early Thomas . . . presupposes a reference of its horrors to
something further. It does not exaggerate; it can barely ap-
proximate the horror of what it symbolizes" (18). What it
symbolizes is the suffering of a sensitive, noble man who
suffers because he has no faith and who understands the consequences of his condition.

II *Character*

At the beginning of this chapter, we observed that Olson
has discovered a progress in Thomas from this darkness to
light. There is no question, however, that the same voice
speaks from all of Thomas' poems; he depicts only one character, most likely himself. In this respect, he is unlike Shakespeare or Browning; but he is like Wallace Stevens or Marianne Moore. Although the range of Thomas' imagination
allows him to enter even into the bodies of animals, he always,
Olson contends, looks out through his own eyes.

Thomas has tremendous capacity for feeling for others,
but it is *his* feeling that matters to him; he does not *suffer* the
feelings of others: "Moved by grief for a burned child, nobly
and powerfully moved as he is, he does not suffer imagina-
tively the experience of the child, does not share in it in the
least; he sees the pain and horror from without, and the resolution he reaches is a resolution for him, not for the child"
(23). Because Thomas depicts only one character who is
capable of only a certain restricted range of feelings, he must,
in Olson's opinion, either achieve the sublime or fail altogether:

When the conception underlying his poem is a powerful lofty
one, and controls all the devices of his poem, Thomas is
magnificent; when the conception is trivial, or when his treatment of it does not sufficiently manifest it, he is utterly
disappointing. His art demands great energy of thought and
passion and all the accoutrements of the grand style; when
the high conception is wanting, energy becomes the melodramatic or the morbid, ecstasy becomes hysteria, and the
high style becomes obscure bombast. (23-24)

Olson illustrates "high conception" with Thomas' "Ballad of the Long-legged Bait," but analysis of this kind of power is one of Olson's oldest interests dating back in print to the 1942 essay on Longinus. The theme of this poem, says Olson, is common enough: "salvation must be won through mortification of the flesh." As the imagination of Thomas refashions this idea, however, it is ennobled:

> The process of purification becomes the strange voyage of the lone fisherman; the bait is "A girl alive with his hooks through her lips"; she is, "all the wanting flesh his enemy," "Sin who had a woman's shape"; and the quarry sought is no less than all that Time and Death have taken; for, since Sin brought Time and Death into the world, the destruction of Sin will restore all that has been lost. With the death of the girl, the sea gives up its dead; Eden returns, "A garden holding to her hand / With birds and animals"; and the sea disappears, accomplishing the prophecy "And there was no more sea." (24)

At the end of the poem, the fisherman has returned to the land, become Eden, with the "heart" he has sacrificed in his hands. I see, along with Olson, a triumph over the flesh, in the poem's conclusion; but I also find a nostalgia in the final quatrain which softens it:

> Good-bye, good luck, struck the sun and the moon,
> To the fisherman lost on the land.
> He stands alone at the door of his home,
> With his long-legged heart in his hand.

There are other poems of Thomas' whose underlying conceptions are, Olson thinks, equally grand and expansive—"Fern Hill," "Poem in October," "A Refusal to Mourn," and, especially, the "Altarwise by Owl-light" sonnets. The voice which speaks from these poems is that of a man of great imagination and feeling who is capable of grand conceptions and who is able to particularize his conceptions so that their full emotional power is exploited.

III *Action*

Olson is at home among his theories of art in his discussion of Thomas; he finds that the actions of Thomas' poems, like those of most lyrics, involve his single character acting by himself in a "closed situation"; no one else is involved. Even in such poems as "I see the boys of summer" in which there is a kind of dialogue, the "dialogue" is simply a device which enables the single character to exhibit with dramatic directness the various aspects of a question or a subject.

Earlier, in Olson's theories of the lyric, three types of activity were outlined: "the simply emotional, the moral but private, and the act itself." Olson proposes that Thomas is "a poet of the internal moral workings of the soul, and that he deals, not with moments, but with complex processes" (33). By "complex," Olson means processes which involve a number of lines of causation which are often in conflict with one another. To choose, as Thomas has, "the dynamic rather than the static . . . the complex rather than the simple, has its consequences for poetic method" (34): Thomas cannot organize a poem around a single image, as can someone who treats of a moment, because there is no progression in a poem which treats of a *moment*.

Moment poems must be analytical in method; and, though the poet dissects the moment ("factors-out" what he wants to use), "the experience," in Olson's words, "is still whole and single, a single idea, a single intuition, a single emotional reaction or sensation" (35). In such instances, a single image, symbol, or metaphor can be used to give unity to the elements of the moment which the poet has chosen to employ. In the "complicated processes" which Thomas imitates in his poems, a succession of images, symbols, and metaphors is necessary to reflect the changing sensations, thoughts, and feelings he depicts.

Olson argues, furthermore, that the processes which Thomas employs are often "dialectically complex" in that his images, symbols, and metaphors are many times "succinct statements of argument." Olson thinks that the romantic notion of Thomas as a rhapsodic, wild Welshman is belied by the intellectual

rigor with which his poems are organized. The poem "I see
the boys of summer," Olson reads as a "terse and complicated
argument about how life ought to be lived" (36). "A process
in the weather of the heart," "Light breaks where no sun
shines," and "The force that through the green fuse drives
the flower" work out man's relationship to the external universe. " 'When once the twilight locks no longer' is a meditation on the origin of the idea of death, terminating in a decision that life is to be lived vigorously" (36).

Complicated as the arguments and statements of the poems
are, Olson thinks that the problem in understanding them
derives from Thomas' presenting simultaneously three conflicting lines of activity: "The process of conscious thought,
the process of the emotions, and the process of the subconscious" (37). "Imagine," Olson suggests, "three files of
people passing through a narrow corridor and pushing against
one another in all directions; you will then have a simplified
parallel to a Dylan Thomas poem" (37). Olson expands this
parallel by saying he uses the word "simplified" because conflict often exists within each of the three lines.

To illustrate a typical Thomas complex of conflicts that involves all three lines of activity, Olson selects "If I were tickled by the rub of love." This poem involves a series of plays
on the word "rub" which is readily associated with Hamlet's
"Aye there's the rub" and with the Queen's line, "the world
is full of rubs," in *Richard II*. The word play takes the form of
punning. The "rubs" on which the poem's speaker meditates
are not only "rubs" in Shakespeare's sense of the word but
also *literal* "rubs." The poem investigates the possibility that
any of the "rubs" can "tickle"; for only *such* a "rub" would be
worth celebrating. In the first four stanzas the speaker says,
in successive subjunctives, that, *if* he were an unborn child
again and were "tickled" by the "rub" of birth, he would not
fear sin, nor its punishment, nor the misery of infancy; *if* he
were "tickled" by the "rub" of growth, he would not fear
violent death from any cause; *if* he were "tickled" by the "desires" of adolescence, he would not fear either sex or the
"grave"; *if* the "rub" of love itself "tickled" him enough, he
would not fear old age nor the "sea of scums" of debauchery.

The point is that the speaker does fear all the things of
which he has spoken. Stanza Five, which Olson quotes and
analyzes, is the key:

> This world is half the devil's and my own,
> Daft with the drug that's smoking in a girl
> And curling round the bud that forks her eye.
> An old man's shank one-marrowed with my bone,
> And all the herrings smelling in the sea,
> I sit and watch the worm beneath my nail
> Wearing the quick away.

He is "daft" with love; he recognizes the old man he must
become in the man he is; the smell of debauchery already is
assailing him; and he can watch death approaching in every
undulation of his pulse. He shares this world with the devil
because, "whatever he fears, he also desires as much as he
fears. What attracts or compels him is also what repels him"
(38). Olson finds subconscious conflict in the fact that, since
life is inseparable from sex, sex is desirable, even compulsive;
but, for all that, sex cannot stifle fear, and is, in Olson's words,
"'associated with sin, senile impotency, pain, and death, and
so undesirable" (38). Even these last qualities, however, because
they are linked with sex, share in its attractiveness and com-
pulsiveness.

On the conscious level, the conflict comes from the awareness that the speaker is simultaneously attracted and repelled and
that he cannot decide whether he *ought* to be attracted by that
which he finds attractive. He is also aware of the compulsion
under which he labors and of the fact that his reason cannot
under any circumstances triumph. Emotional conflict arises both
from the conscious process of thought and from the subconscious. Reason—which balances each "ought" with an "ought
not," each possibility with an impossibility—generates conflicting feelings. Meanwhile, the subconscious drives toward
and away from sex produce concurrently hope and fear.
Moreover, Olson concludes, the emotions generated by each
source are in conflict with each other. The poem concludes on
the note—only life itself is worth celebrating: "I would be
tickled by the rub that is: / Man be my metaphor."

IV *Techniques of Depiction*

Olson turns at this point from a discussion of "what" Thomas depicts to that which, as I have noted at least twice before, is perhaps more important in practical criticism: "how" he depicts. In fact, Olson has been talking of "what" chiefly in terms of depiction. Thomas uses two chief variations of narrative manner which Olson calls *pseudo-drama* and *pseudo-narrative*. In general, pseudo-drama results when something which is not true drama is represented as if it were: the poet causes the real speaker in the poem to assume the mask, or masks, of someone else as part of the representative device. Olson illustrates Thomas' use of pseudo-drama:

> Among Thomas' pseudo-dramatic dialogues are "I see the boys of summer," "Find meat on bones," and "If my head hurt a hair's foot"; the "masks" in these are, respectively, "the boys of summer" and the person criticizing them; the father and the son; the unborn child and its mother. Instances of pseudo-dramatic monologue are "before I knocked," "My world is pyramid," and "When once the twilight locks no longer"; the mask in the first one is Jesus, in the second "the secret child," in the third the spirit; but all are mouth-pieces of the Thomasian hero. (43)

Pseudo-drama has many of the advantages of true drama: it causes a gain in directness and vividness; and, as Olson observes, it "can heighten the contrast between two opposing points of view, or between conflicting motives and desires, and it can produce a striking degree of economy as well" (43). Olson uses "If my head hurt a hair's foot" for illustration. The bare statement of the poem's contents involves a series of hypothetical propositions: the unborn child would rather not be born *if* it knew what suffering its birth would give to its mother; however, *if* the mother was aware of the child's awareness, she would tell the child it must be born, as Olson says, and "suffer life." By casting the poem in the form of a dialogue, Thomas removes the hypothetical and actualizes the thought.

The term "pseudo-narrative" implies that the speaker in

the poem is narrating about persons who are masks for his own thoughts, feelings, and characteristics, and the two chief poems which employ this device are the "Altarwise by Owl-light" sonnets and the "Ballad of the Long-legged Bait." At this juncture, Olson makes some theoretical statements which parallel those he made in connection with true dramatic representation and representative devices in general. All such devices involve the selection of those parts of the activity the poem imitates which must be represented for the proper effect: the arrangement of the parts of the activity in their most powerful order, and so on.

Olson makes the point that, like the dramatist and the novelist who are concerned with grand plots, the lyricist may represent only part of his lyric action; all of that action; or, in cases where some kind of exposition is necessary, more than that action. Olson says Thomas's variation of procedure depends on the needs of the poem. He cites "Over Sir John's Hill" as an example of a poem with an exposition; "The force that through the green fuse drives the flower" as one which exhibits only its proper action; and "If I were tickled by the rub of love" as one which begins after the action has begun.

If Thomas is variable about the portion of a poem's activity that he represents, he is quite constant in practicing what Olson calls "a quite peculiar characteristic . . . *circumstantial ambiguity*" (45). Because it is difficult to tell "who is saying what or doing what to whom in what circumstances" in a Thomas poem, Olson compares Thomas' practice to that of a playwright who would omit the title of his play; would fail to indicate the time and place; would not assign speeches to characters; and would not provide either a cast or stage directions. Olson gives a new and interesting answer as to why Thomas employs ambiguity: obscurity, where it is not used simply for its own sake and, hence, illegitimately, is a device for forcing the reader to pay close attention. Olson feels that the understanding a reader has to earn, if it is important, provides a reward proportionate to the effort expended. "The poet," he says, "who tantalizes us in order to make us read more closely, and so understand more perfectly and react more completely to, a piece that is delicately and subtly made is perfectly within his rights. He is entitled to the attention he demands, and he rewards us handsomely at the end . . ." (47).

An older answer, which Olson considers more important, depends on his theory of emotions. The emotions a reader feels at any given point, Olson always contends, are a function of the amount and kind of information he possesses. The poet, therefore, controls the reader's emotions by concealing and by revealing information about his characters and their situation. Withholding information creates suspense; and suspense, though not an emotion but a tension, heightens emotions. The same is true of the "unexpected" which results when the reader has been led to think things are of a certain order because something has been suppressed which, when it becomes known, reverses his opinion.

Olson concludes his treatment of Thomas' techniques of depiction with another sally at "The Ballad of the Long-legged Bait." Of this poem, which was first considered in terms of its *action* which Olson said was "a meditation . . . on the possibility of salvation through the mortification of the flesh" (51), Olson observes that the order in which the tale is unfolded leads us through "curiosity (about the peculiarities of the departure), wonder, astonished horror, bewilderment, regret (at the marvelous voyage, the strange bait, the pity of her condition, the enigmatic actions of the fisherman and what happens to the bait) and resignation to a surprised delight (as we learn what the girl signified and what her death means" (51). The representation, Olson explains, fixes directly on the object of imitation, the process of the mortification, which it exhibits symbolically by means of the voyage which is reported by a narrator, who, using the fisherman as a mask, doesn't explain his thought, but knows the significance of the voyage and can, and does, comment, until, at the end, the pieces fall into place.

V *Thomas' Use of Language*

Olson begins the analysis of Thomas' characteristic methods of handling language with the flat statement that the greatest difficulty in reading him arises from the extreme obscurity of his diction. When a poet is as difficult to understand as Thomas is, the tendency of most criticism is to substitute paraphrase for structural analysis; and, though Olson provides a number of paraphrases for various reasons, he rejects the idea that they are any more than a preliminary to criticism, or that they are the best solution to the verbal difficulties of Thomas. Instead, Olson proposes that an illustrated list of the kinds of things Thomas does with words, metaphors, and syntax will provide the reader with the best tools with which to approach the poems.

Thomas likes words, Olson contends, with "multiple meanings and multiple syntactic functions":

> "My world is pyramid" plays on various meanings of the word "fellow" which can be a noun meaning a person, partner, friend, or companion; an adjective meaning associate, accompanying, etc., and a verb with similar meanings. Again the sonnets play upon words like "wether," "weather," "rung" (like a bell), "rung" (of a ladder) . . . where there is similarity of sound only . . .
>
> Sometimes he wants simultaneous meanings, of a multiple meaning word; in "A grief ago," the phrase "boxed into love" has simultaneous meanings; as Thomas himself declared, ' "boxed' has the coffin and the pug-glove in it." He will mix levels or kinds of language most startlingly, current with archaic, literary with slang and thieves' lingo. For instance, in "Because the pleasure-bird whistles" the term "bum city" means Sodom which was a bad city . . . where Sodomy was practiced, so that we have both the slang and vulgar meanings of "bum"; let me add that the people of Sodom were undoubtedly "bums" in at least two senses . . . Thomas will also effect parody through the use of similar words: "minstrel angles" for "ministering angels," "maid and head" for "maidenhead." (54-55)

As for Thomas' metaphors, Olson says they are troublesome because the ground of likeness is so often very obscure, sometimes only a forced resemblance, or only such a resemblance as would be fancied by someone in a particular mood or frame of mind. Thomas likes, also, to make metaphors appear self-contradictory or to mix them; and the result is that his metaphors often appear to be "enigmas or riddles." Thomas, Olson continues, unlike the metaphysical poets whom he resembles, does not make clear "the grounds for his fantastic comparisons and analogies" (56).

Olson classifies the metaphors of Thomas under six general categories, each of which he illustrates. First, there is the "self-contradictory" metaphor: "In 'Our eunuch dreams,' . . . we have 'one-dimensioned ghosts.' 'Ghosts' here is itself a metaphor for images on a movie screen; but how are these one-dimensioned'? Thomas returns to the metaphor in the succeeding section of the poem, in the lines 'The photograph is married to the eye, / Grafts on its bride one-sided skins of truth,' and we realize that what he meant by 'one-dimensioned' is 'one-sided'; there is no further side to a photograph or a movie image" (56). The point is that "one-dimensioned" is not to be taken literally but is itself a metaphor.

Second, in some metaphors Thomas is deceptive about what he is likening to what. Olson draws his example from "Like a running grave" which contains the metaphor "time tracks you down." The immediate reaction is simply to read this as a metaphor from hunting; but we find in the last stanza that time is "also being analogized to a runner on a cinder track who . . . shapes an oval, an 'O,' standing for the nothingness of death" (57).

The third kind of metaphor Olson calls the "metaphor of logical consequence." Such metaphors always contain some "supposition or allusion" which provides the ground of likeness as a logical consequence: In "In my Craft or Sullen Art," " 'Ivory stages' means 'stages whereon people act falsely like actors'; it involves an allusion to the Virgilian gates of ivory and of horn through which the false and the true dreams, respectively, come" (57).

The fourth class of metaphors are those composite ones in which "the parts are unintelligible until we grasp the whole": "The opening stanza of 'It is the sinner's dust-tongued bell' is likely to mean little or nothing unless the reader realizes that the details add up to a Black Mass being celebrated, with Satan officiating as priest, and that Time is being compared to Satan executing this office" (58).

The fifth type of metaphor, which presents very little trouble, results from compounding; and it needs no explanation except when it contains an ambiguity. "Lamb white days" and a "springful of larks" are clear enough; "the farm at its white trades" is not quite so immediate, though, once the meaning of "white" is guessed, it clearly enough means the work of the farm in snow time.

The sixth and last type of metaphor Olson describes as "implied or suggested." He cites the metaphor from "The Ballad of the Long-legged Bait" in which the storm (part of the whole symbolic structure of the poem) is likened to a supernatural warship, although no direct mention of such a ship is made. Another variety of this class of metaphors results from altering a stock phrase so that it either becomes a metaphor or, if it is already one, has the ground of likeness altered. The substitution of "a jaw for news" for "a nose for news" is an example of the latter; in the substitution of "the stations of the breath" for "the stations of the cross," "breath" (life) is likened by implication to Christ's journey to Calvary.

Thomas also employs the circumlocutions of periphrasis in ways which often involve metaphor. Olson thinks Thomas sometimes sounds like "one of the Welsh enigmatic poets of the fourteenth century." For example, the line "Because the pleasure-bird whistles after hot wires' means 'Because the song-bird sings more sweetly after being blinded with red-hot wires or needles.'" Or "'A wind that plucked a goose' means 'a wind full of snow like goose-feathers'" (59). Moreover such miscellaneous metaphorical devices as kennings (wind-well" for "source of wind") and "primitive definitions" ("bow and arrow birds" for "weathercocks") involve some kind of recognition; but they present no great difficulty.

The final complexity in Thomas' language is syntactical. Olson lists several grammatical pitfalls and gives examples of each. He calls them "ambiguous reference," "false parallelism," "ellipsis," "false apposition," and "delayed complement":

To take these in turn: In "Half of the fellow father as he doubles

/ His sea-sucked Adam in the hollow hulk," what is the grammatical reference of "he"; and what part of speech is "fellow"? [As Olson's note, p. 99, makes clear, father and noun.] In "Oh miracle of fishes! The long dead bite!," is "bite" verb or noun? (Constant playing upon phrases like "long-legged bait" suggests that it is a noun, whereas it is a verb; an instance of false parallelism.) In "When, like a running grave" there is an ellipsis of "when" from the second and third lines of the first stanza and from the first line of the second stanza, so that the reader is baffled what to put with what. Here is "false apposition":

> I damp the waxlights in your tower dome.
> Joy is the knock of dust, Cadaver's shoot
> Or bud of Adam through his boxy shift,
> Love's twilit nation and the skull of state,
> Sir, is your doom.

The reader tends to read "Love's twilit nation, etc.," as an appositive, whereas it is not. As to the "delayed complement," in the first stanza of "Poem in October" many words intervene between "hearing" and its infinitive object "beckon" and many again between "beckon" and its object "myself" (60-61).

To complete the discussion of Thomas' language, Olson asks what did Thomas mean by saying, as he often did, that he wanted to be read literally when he is so obviously symbolic and metaphorical? Olson thinks that Thomas was trying to avoid the critic who would come to his work with hypotheses which would cause him to *impose* rather than *find* meaning.

VI Altarwise by Owl-light

Olson's analysis of Thomas' magnificent, strange sonnets has occasioned both the greatest praise and the strongest distaste. The reviewer in the *Times Literary Supplement* asserted that Olson was the first critic to have made sense of the sonnets; but Ralph Maud, when he reviewed the book as late as 1963[7], was dismayed by what he considered the excessive

ingenuity of Olson's explications. Maud's objections seem
niggling, and he certainly has nothing to offer on the sonnets
which is impressive. Monroe Beardsley (he and his colleague
W. K. Wimsatt are professional Olson baiters) undertakes the
easy task of accusing Olson of *imposing* his views on the sonnets without offering an alternative view or really showing
Olson to be wrong at any important point.[8] It is indeed possible to read the sonnets in other ways than Olson has; for
H. H. Kleinman has written a book about them which makes
very little use of Olson's work.[9] Kleinman's interpretations are
plausible in many instances but he is often too far from the
text. Olson's interpretation accounts for more of the obscure
details of the text than any other interpretation I have seen.
What is more, the action of the poem, as seen in Olson's reading, is cosmic both in its grandeur and its implications for
mankind.

Olson identifies six levels of symbolism in the sonnets:

> (1) a level based on the analogy of human life to the
> span of a year, which permits the use of phenomena of the
> seasons to represent events of human life, and vice versa;
> (2) a level based on an analogy between the sun and
> man, permitting the attributes of each to stand for those of
> the other:
> (3) a level of Thomas' "private" symbolism:
> (4) a level based on ancient myth, principally Greek,
> representing the fortunes of the sun in terms of the adventures
> of the sun-hero Hercules;
> (5) a level based on relations of the *constellation* Her-
> cules to other constellations and astronomical phenomena;
> and;
> (6) a level derived from the Christian interpretation
> of levels 4 and 5. (64)

The first two of these levels, Olson says, are without difficulty;
while the third can be understood in terms of what he has
already said about Thomas' "private" symbolism; but the last
three require explanation—and on them his reading of the
sonnets is chiefly founded.

I shall not restate Olson's analysis other than to say he explains the details of the poem with considerable clarity by relating them to the march of the constellations, especially that of Hercules, across the heavens. In Thomas' use of the star-filled skies as the symbolic spaces through which his hero proceeds from horror to hope, the poet employs the meanings the Greeks assigned to the stars; those that Christian writers later assigned to them; and some of the poet's own devising. The magnificence of the hope which the hero achieves is proportionate to the profundity of his despair, and the shape of both are made available by the immensities—the intergalactic reaches—against which they are felt.

The intellectual, emotional, and moral process that this poem's hero undergoes is clearly a serious one. It is also clear that the "strange legend of the sonnets" with its symbolic action is a proper vehicle to set "powerfully and quickly before us the state of mind of the man contemplating . . . The images tell, step by step, a painful story, in which the heaven he had once hoped for spells out nothing but his doom, until the message is complete, and he realizes that sin, the venom of the Serpent, is to a merciful God nothing but the necessary condition of mercy" (87).

To conclude the book, Olson says that he has so great a respect for the work of Thomas that he may often have been led into eulogy rather than criticism. He thinks, however, that to state the facts about the best of Thomas' poetry is to eulogize; for "the best" is all that really matters. Olson is fully aware that contemporary criticism has only the first word about a poet, but he believes that to be an important word. He finds great poems in each of the three periods—poems which Olson thinks will endure. In the first period, there are "I see the boys of summer," "The force that through the green fuse drives the flower," "If I were tickled by the rub of love," "Especially when the October wind," "Light breaks where no sun shines," "Foster the light," "And death shall have no dominion," and perhaps his greatest work, the sonnets. In the second period: "A Refusal to Mourn" and "This Side of the Truth." Finally, in the third period: "Poem in October," "A Winter's Tale," "Vision and Prayer," the "Ballad of the Long-legged Bait," and "Fern Hill."

CHAPTER *8*

Elder Olson, Poet: Early Poems

I *Backgrounds*

THE late Yvor Winters wrote of R. S. Crane in a passage aimed at all the Chicago Critics: "He seems in brief to have come to poetry through an interest in criticism, rather than to criticism through an interest in poetry."[1] Winter's remark, aside from its preciosity, is far wide of its mark as it is aimed at Elder Olson. Elder Olson published his first poems at the age of nineteen in the May, 1928, issue of *Poetry: A Magazine of Verse* and a good ten years before his first serious critical work: the study of general prosody that became his doctoral dissertation. Considering that Winters finds that the essence of poetry is verse, it is ironic that Olson, whose knowledge of metrics is so much deeper than Winters', went so far beyond the study of prosody in *his* understanding of poetry. One of the most noteworthy aspects of Olson's earliest poems—though an even more marked characteristic in his first collection, *Thing of Sorrow*—is his facility with fresh and flexible metrical forms.

Olson's earliest poems are not great ones; but, from the perspective of his later work, they can be seen to contain the beginnings of the talent which was to produce some of the most serious and important modern lyrics and at least two fine plays. The following excerpt from the first published poem, "Soft Music," despite its Shelleyian inversions, has a toughness which Shelley who could "die," "faint," and "fail" for love never achieved:

> I suddenly knew
> That somewhere, afar, beyond windless skies,

> Beyond the poor hearts and eyes of man,
> You were asleep. And the heart of you
> Was stiller than moss in a darkened wood,
> Or stones buried deep in the river's bed,
> Or grief in the heart's pale solitude.
> And you were asleep, and you were dead.[2]

And, just two years later, Olson published "Dirge for a White Bird," the first poem in which he showed his mastery of the imagery of winter, a mastery which has grown steadily and which has produced poems which dazzle the sight with an effect of pure sunlight on ice while they freeze the heart with terror. I am thinking here especially of the following poems, though there are many more in which snow falls with beautiful effects: "Spring Ghost," "Winter Nightfall," and "The Last Entries in the Journal."

In addition to Olson's precision with the imagery of winter, he is at ease with all the seasons; his poems image the weathers, the objects, and the creatures of nature with great felicity. In the earliest poems, Olson also indicated that he possessed the wry humor which was to find later and more serious expression in "Plot Improbable, Character Unsympathetic," "Punch and Judy Songs," "Directions to the Armorer," and "The Side of the Bread." In these late poems, the humor, like that in *Hamlet*, tends to underline the horror and irony they convey. In the early "Angle Worms," however, the humor, like that of Ogden Nash or Eliot's *Book of Practical Cats*, is there for its own sake: "All angleworms, however able, / Are sexually somewhat unstable."[3]

The most important type among the youthful poems is what I call "the imagistic lyric of ideas," a kind of poem which Olson has continued to write throughout the years with increasing skill and importance. At this point, I shall say only of these poems—other than to name two of them, "Essay on Deity" and "Talisman of Words"—that, concerned with thought though they are, they are neither didactic (as Olson defines the didactic) nor unfeeling. Rather, they are poems which present circumstances (primarily depicted in images, including the wintry ones already mentioned) which evoke specific thoughts and feelings which attend the possibility of their truth.

Before considering Olson's first book of poems, *Thing of Sorrow,* I want to dispose of one of the most persistent charges made against him: that he sounds like all the poets he has read. From the beginning, reviewers have found echoes of Donne, Shelley, Baudelaire, Hopkins, Browning, Yeats, Aiken, Eliot, MacLeish, and Thomas, among others, in Olson's work. The chief complainant, though he is by no means alone, was the late Randall Jarrell. Jarrell, who was especially disturbed by Olson's long poem, *The Cock of Heaven* (1940), pointed out in his review[4] that several of its parts appeared to be direct imitations of both the early and late Yeats; that he often sounded like Browning; and that in one place he had borrowed the structure of Eliot's *Animula,* and, in another, that of the choruses of *Murder in the Cathedral.*

As late as 1955 in a review of *The Scarecrow Christ,* Jarrell sang much the same song: "Elder Olson seems to know the world only through literature. They [his poems] are best when he deliberately assumes a manner and the properties that go with it . . . when he writes a poem in his own style it is a stagey, exaggerated mixture of other people's poetry."[5]

Olson has never denied the echoes in his work; and, writing of the method of *The Cock of Heaven* in 1963, he said that, "To emphasize the permanence of the problems (those at the heart of the poem), I thought it might be effective to represent different voices discussing them in all ages, in a kind of simultaneous colloquy. This device necessitated the use of quotation both overt and hidden, allusion, and frequently direct imitation."[6]

The echoes in Olson's poetry are not troubling. In fact, the echoes are an asset because he is often better than the poet he is echoing and because, in spite of their familiar quality, his poems have their own special brand of originality. Just what the originality is Olson has treated metaphorically in a recent piece, "The Exposition of the Quarrel of the Birds," the subject matter of which is the varieties of criticism: "The

quarrel is . . . / Between those who hold that the mockingbird / Has no voice of its own, and those who observe
/ That no other bird has the voice of the mockingbird."[7]

It may be true, as James Dickey says,[8] that Olson had
Thomas' "The Ballad of the Long-legged Bait" in mind when
he wrote "The Ballad of the Scarecrow Christ," but the poems
are so different in content (that which each imitates) that
comparisons are critically irrelevant. Olson is a great believer
in the idea that a poet can avail himself of whatever means
have been developed in a particular art. For example, hear
what he says about the lyric in the twentieth century:
". . . the technical resources of the lyric poet have never
been greater, . . . devices exist for nearly everything the modern
poet wishes to say."[9]

II Thing of Sorrow

Thing of Sorrow (1934),[10] the first collection of Olson's poems,
attracted considerable attention as the work of a young poet
who showed exceptional promise. The book won the Friends of
Literature Award for 1935, and no less imposing a figure than
William Rose Benet wrote that "Elder Olson's book is important;
and yet it is likely to be overlooked in the presence of work by
other young poets of the day. It is important to me because of
its metaphysical properties and because of the distinguished
beauty of its writing. Indeed, Mr. Olson writes with so rare a
distinction, albeit he has no great range as yet, that he awakens
new hope for American poetry."[11]

The remarks of reviewers, both pro and con, usually need to be
discounted on the grounds that they are necessarily hasty; but
I found no wholly unfavorable review. Said P. M. J. in the
New York Times (Oct. 14, 1934), "Mr. Olson's brief book
of poems is a promise of authentic lyrical talent"; Marion
Stroebel in *The Chicago Daily Tribune* (Dec. 14, 1934), "Elder
Olson has as sensitive an ear as any lyric poet writing today";
E. L. Walton in *Books* (Oct. 7, 1934), "This is by no means
a book to be neglected, for Mr. Olson has a real gift especially
in the handling of unusual rhythms." Finally, G. M. S. in the
Boston Transcript (Oct. 10, 1934); "So much beauty and feeling

are here that there is no room for morbidity or futility." That the fame of its author has not grown proportionately as he fulfilled the high promise is not only ironic but also another story.

Thing of Sorrow is a slight book of twenty-three lyrics, thirteen of which Olson in his mature judgment has reprinted in the latest collection of his poems. Several of the poems of *Thing of Sorrow* had been printed earlier in *Poetry*, among them, "Talisman of Words" and "Essay on Deity." All of the poems are typical lyrics in that they involve a single character acting in a closed situation. Furthermore, the character in a poem is valued on the basis of the kind of thought and feeling he has; these necessarily reveal his moral stature by implication if not directly.[12] In these poems there are, I think, two voices distinct enough from each other to be meaningfully differentiated; abstracted, however, from the poems in which they speak, they could be considered to be two sides of the same personality.

One of the voices belongs to a young man who, like most young men, has experienced the sweet despair of early love which has been lost and which he realizes, moreover, was an ideal incompatible with reality. This speaker is admirable not only for his ability to convey the "way love was" but also to refrain from being maudlin about it. We hear this voice in "Prelude to Despair," "The Ghostly Spring," "Madrigal," "The Strange Summer," "Arabesque" and "Novel in Pictures."

The second voice, also clearly that of a young man because of its intensity, is a thoughtful one. He to whom it belongs speaks of such concepts as pantheism ("Essay on Deity"); idealism ("To Man");[13] the relationship of body and soul ("MS. Unearthed at Delos," "The Changeling," "Catechism at Midnight," "Colloquy,"); the power of words ("Talisman of Words"); the nature of time ("Calendar");[14] Descarte's vortices and death ("Elegy"); *ubi sunt* ("Dirge"); Plato's doctrine of reminiscence ("Children"); the loss of youth ("Spring Ghost"); and man and his earth ("The Tale"). The second speaker earns esteem because he treats concepts that are all important ones and because he provides the right particulars in his poems to convey them with great power. His weakness—one he loses as Elder Olson matures—is a kind of naiveté which produces, at points, an intellectual brashness.

One of the poems, "Novel in Pictures," employs the device of *pseudo-narrative* in that its speaker uses the "he" of the poem as a mask through which to voice his own thoughts and feelings; and, though in rudimentary form, the brief and exquisite "Colloquy" is *pseudo-drama*. The activities depicted in the poems of *Thing of Sorrow* usually involve their speakers in moments of thought or feeling. Only one poem, it seems to me, is concerned with a process, rather than a moment; and it is "Novel in Pictures." This poem conveys the process of the passage from childhood to young manhood in a series of imagistic vignettes, each of which depicts a stage in that process. As with "Novel in Pictures," the chief depictive of all the poems is imagery, both with and without metaphor and symbol. The imagery is most often aimed at producing precise images or sensations—at producing its objects without modification, though rarely for the sake of those objects in themselves. Rather, the images in a given poem, and the thoughts and feelings which accompany them, are aimed at the overall effect the poem seeks to achieve. They sometimes, hence, tell primarily of the intellectual qualities of the speaker, or they provide circumstances from which thought and feeling can be evoked.

All of the poems show a great facility with prosody, and many of their meters seem based as much on quantity as on stress. For example, "Children" has twenty-five stress stanzas and a multiplicity of monosyllables; and its lines, despite the ordered variations in the number of stresses, occupy approximately equal amounts of time. This command of rhythm, still a great strength in Olson's work, is understandable in a young poet who had just surrendered the idea of being a concert pianist and to whom the "quantities" of music must have been only too familiar. As already mentioned, this command of metrics is documented in the doctoral dissertation on general prosody which Olson wrote just a few years later.

Of each of the kinds of poems I have been describing, those which deal with love, and those which treat ideas, the two illustrations which I have chosen—"The Strange Summer" and "Calendar"—are not necessarily the best poems of their types in *Thing of Sorrow*; but each has a special excellence and is quite representative. "The Strange Summer" displays the unreasonableness of young love, and it evokes the feeling of tremendous frustration and disbelief that only complete rejection can evoke. The "he" of the poem is a mask for the speaker who is looking back with the recognition that his sense of "loss" was more for himself than for the beloved. Though this is an early poem, as is "Calendar," "The Strange Summer" is a good example of Olson's skill with the imagery of the seasons and weathers:

> He who is loved no longer
> And loves still beyond reason
> Is like one who would constrain summer
> Past summer's season.
>
> Incredulous, he hears the gale.
> It is the thrush, he cries. The snow
> Falls, he stares, he rages,
> He will not have it so.
>
> He goes distraught through the stark wood.
> It is summer, he cries. No cry avails him.
> In frenzy he puts back dead leaves to their branches
> Till the cold fells him. (19)

Though the experience depicted is a youthful one, it is definitely universal; and the insight it contains about the nature of human relations; or at least what possibly may be behind them, is chilling. But Olson has depicted a similar insight with consummate skill within the last few years—thirty years after "The Strange Summer"—in "Mirror," a poem which, with only one direct statement, suggests the serpent and, perhaps, the nature of what happened to man in Eden. The speaker in this poem is no boy—he is a man whose clarity of vision is appalling:

> The gown falls fold on fold
> Sway in those burnished coils,
> Lift your delicate head,
> Lean to your mirror, stare
> Into those brilliant eyes
> Till they grow dark and bleak.
> This is not vanity,
> Disliking what you see;

> Gaze on: you too surmise
> The bitter secret there.
> Press your hand to your breast,
> You too are appalled:
> What you thought your love
> Was nothing but the cold,
> The ravaging inner cold,
> That drives the wilderness snake
> Into the woodsman's bed.[15]

In "The Tale" there are some lines which are relevant to the burden of "Calendar": "We pursued / Down immaterial / Autumn and ghostly spring / Time's wraith, the phantom year" . . . (3). The concept with which "Calendar" deals is that, however evanescent the seasons are and however partial our observation of them is, the revolving seasons and things like them are what make us aware of the passage of time. There is a suggestion, too, that time may be wholly subjective. We find again the precise imagery of the seasons, and we observe the geometric qualities of the poem: how its January beginning softens to spring, warms to summer, matures to autumn, and ends in December. The poignancy and nostalgia of the poem result, equally from the concept it treats, and from the beauty of the seasons which revolve so rapidly and so few times in our lives. The "they" of the poem is everyone:

> Always in the clean winter, in blue snow,
> The oak sighed, moving in sere leaf still.
> They could see the frame town now through
>   the stripped trees.
> Easter came with snow still on the wooden
>   steeple.
> The month the woods would drip ceaselessly
>   in the thaw.
>
> Later they saw glass rain reflecting the
>   green
> —The windmills, the red barns, the orchards
>   glimmering through.
> Afterward beyond the ploughed dark
> Earth the Rain-Ring stood against deep sky.

Noons in the weighted shine saw the
      gilt
Cock at the roof-peak, at the apex of slant
      shingles.
Always the elms would be motioning at the
      window,
And the coloured fruits silently loosening
      amid leaves.

Autumn would be clouds and the crows' cry
Blown over hard fields, the woods deep with
                        cast
Leaf, and red frost at dawn in the rutted
Sand road past the covered bridge.

At the year's end, winter: the burning emblems
Beyond the wind, bright snow in the lit
Branches, the dumb sightless
Moon wandering above the rim of the dead
                        planet;

They knew they would wake one day and the
            year be gone. (25)

In summary, *Thing of Sorrow* is a remarkable first volume
of verses in which Olson gave definite evidences of the prosodic
skill, depictive techniques, controlled feelings, and depth of conception which dominate his later work.

III   The Cock of Heaven

Six years after *Thing of Sorrow* there appeared what I can
only consider a tactical mistake in Elder Olson's campaign to
become a famous poet, *The Cock of Heaven*.[16] Even those reviewers most disposed to be friendly were hard pressed to say
good things about it. One review in particular, that in *Time
Magazine* for November 18, 1940, was the most damaging. Not
only did it hurt the book at which it was directed, but the fact
that *Time* has never since reviewed a book of Elder Olson's
is also significant. For all the superficial glibness of its reviewers, *Time* has influence enough to make or break young

poets. In the following quotation from the *Time* review, the preciosity is self-evident:

> *The Cock of Heaven* is a long poem about the irremediable genesis, incorrigible exodus, and appalling exeunt of the God-damned, salvation-proof children of Adam . . .
>
> *The Cock of Heaven* is craftily written, and its theme is major, but it fails to be more than backhanded poetry. It produced in its reader's conscience nothing more quickening than the kind of agitation that would follow his discovery that the skeleton in his closet was a corpse.

We have already mentioned Randall Jarrell's *New Republic* review for November 11, 1940, which took Olson to task for his borrowings. *Living Age* called the book "Technically smart, but unoriginal." And John Holmes in the *Atlantic* for February, 1941, had this to say: "In spite of the elaborate preparation, the book remains a book from which a limited number of people will get good, and a book in which, for all the lyric skill of which Olson is a minor master, there is not the simplicity which one seeks in poetry."

It is hardly perceptive to insist that poetry to be good must be "simple," but "elaborateness" *can* be a fault. I do not know how seriously Olson took these reviews, but they must have been disconcerting after the labor of writing such a poem and after the favorable reviews of his first book. Perhaps the most disconcerting thing was the recognition that, as a whole, the poem was a failure. In any case, Olson published no more books of poems for fourteen years. This long silence accounts in part for the fact that his work as a poet has not had wider recognition.

There is no question but that the concepts behind *The Cock of Heaven* are too elaborate; nor that its execution is uneven and, in places, melodramatic. Lines like the following, however accurately they convey the repulsiveness of sloth, are too macabre:

> Because of my much flesh and the dropsical sickness
> It was my wont to ride the palace round,
> In affable weathers, propped in a gold chair

Borne by sixteen eunuchs, and attended
By twenty excellent horsemen clad in brass.
Nevertheless the whole proved insufficient:
As we descended from the hall of bronze
One Marius, a disappointed captain,
Knelt on the palace-roof and cast his sword
Whirling like a wheel of fire; and I could not fend myself
But it took arm and head; and the trunk toppled;
And ropes of blood rolled ravelling over the stairs. (21)

The elaborate concepts behind *The Cock of Heaven* are what give rise to the excesses in it. As the note which Olson prefixed to the poem says: "*The Cock of Heaven* is a poem in the form of a commentary on a text. The text itself might be called an epitome of human history; consequently, the commentary has the character of an historical summation. Book I deals with the destruction of the world, and the causes of both creation and destruction; Books II–VIII deal with the seven wanderings of humanity; and Book IX deals with the universal catastrophe."

The "text" upon which the poem comments, the "epitome of human history," identifies the cock which crowed when Peter denied Christ with the one which announced the birth of Christ from the dish of Herod and both of them with the Angel Gabriel who sat in the forbidden tree in Eden to warn Adam and Eve and who will announce the end of the world. Furthermore, says the text, the cock of final doom will crow in a time of great persecution of the Jews (the crematoriums of Nazi Germany were burning brightly as the poem was written) and of "intestine wars" (World War II was in the making) when the Devil becomes so sickened with the world's filth that he surrenders and when Judas, through complete repentance, has become as sanctified as Christ.

At that time, too, Ahasuerus, the wandering Jew, will return home; and the Magi, whose presence in the world saved it from the wrath of God, will die. For not even the seven messiahs who were sent to combat the seven sins, nor Christ, who was said to have cast out all seven, has been successful. "The seven wanderings of humanity" treated in Books II through VIII are the Seven Deadly Sins that still dominate the world. Because they do, man is clearly damned; and the sign of his damnation is the fact that the tree of Eden was cut down and made into the cross of Christ and that the site of Eden itself became Calvary. Furthermore, all man's sins spring from his mortality; and the eating of forbidden fruit is only a parable of "some question concerning death that could not be asked of God, which Man yet asked; and all our anguish is the answer." Finally, the only salvation lies in God's being born into the world; but even that event will make it worthy only of destruction.

Olson says in a note to the *Collected Poems* of 1963 that the method of *The Cock of Heaven* is that of the Scholastics: "statement of question, division of question, argument and counterargument." I am, however, unable to see how this statement applies either to individual lyrics or to larger segments of the poem. Such an understanding might make for a clearer recognition of the organizing principles of the individual sections. Olson also clearly says that he has sought to deal with the nature of man and with "certain moral problems, as well as problems of guilt and innocence" by discussing them in a series of related but independent short poems. This technique becomes confusing, however, because the independent lyrics of the poem are essentially imitative; though taken together, they become the "argument" of a didactic poem which presents a philosophic position, just as Lucretius and Dante did.

To summarize and to lead to the real value of *The Cock of Heaven*, two reviews of the poem, both still fresh and basically right after nearly thirty years, are important. One is by the poet, teacher, and editor of *Poetry, A Magazine of Verse*, Henry Rago, whose sudden death in the spring of 1969 was a shock to all who knew and repected him; the other is by poet-critic Louis Untermeyer. Henry Rago thought that Olson had gone overboard in the melodramatic quality of the poem but that he "always knows what he is about . . . What he has is not simply an ear for language; it is a swiftness and neatness in the manipulation of plot, a competence at really distinguished parody, and an intellectual gift for sharp aphorism."[17] Untermeyer echoes Rago on the stagy pretentiousness of the piece but agrees that, when Olson is writing his best verse, "The reader can afford to forget the pretentious structure, and give his attention to the individual lyrics. There is not only dexterity but vigor in the separate poems which run from fiercely ironic to quietly mystical."[18]

The consensus of opinion is that *The Cock of Heaven* contains many lovely lyrics but that, as a single poem, it simply attempts too much. It appears that Olson has adopted pretty much this opinion himself because in his *Collected Poems,* he has selected twenty-five of the lyrics from *The Cock of Heaven;* and he says: "I have chosen to break up the single long poem, salvaging parts which still interested me . . ."[19]

"Anthropos" from Book I; "Abailard Sleeps at His Book" from Book II (Sloth); Part vii, "The Crusade," from Book III (Guile); Part iv from Book V (Lust); "Imago Mortis" from Book VII (Pride); "Gian Maria Concerning Death" from Book VIII (Anger), and "Winter Marketplace" and "The Christmas Meditation" from Book IX are worthy of attention.

CHAPTER 9

Elder Olson, Poet: Middle and Later Poems and Plays

1 The Scarecrow Christ

THE reception accorded Olson's third book of poems, *The Scarecrow Christ* (1954),[1] was a good deal more friendly than that of *The Cock of Heaven*. The reviews, though far short of recognizing the importance of the book, and with the exception of that of Randall Jarrell of which I spoke in the preceding chapter, were quite favorable. Louise Bogan remarked in *The New Yorker* for April 30, 1955, that Olson's "skill with strict and formal lyric forms is marked, and his diction and imagery are often startlingly precise." Hayden Carruth in *Poetry* (June, 1955), wrote that "One of his best devices is the rather nervous consolidation of detail, as in 'Anthropos,' which may be boring until one is seized by the emerging concept. Some of the later pieces in the book are dramatic conversations and soliloquies which seem to have been published apart from their necessary contexts. But all told the book is quite the opposite of padded and contains poems which no one should be willing to overlook." Louis Untermeyer in the June 18, 1955, issue of *Saturday Review* was even kinder: "The third section is full of unusual concepts matched by appropriately powerful images. It is a highly personal idiom which Mr. Olson employs, alternately melodious, colloquially casual, and darkly menacing."

After the two opening sections of *The Scarecrow Christ*, in which there are poems from Olson's first two books, comes that third section which Untermeyer praised. There are twenty-three poems in Section III, and Olson identifies them as a selection of his work since 1939. All twenty-three of these poems belong, in one sense or another, to that class of Olson's poems which I have labeled the "imagistic lyric of ideas."

Though the voice heard in all these poems is that of the same character, a mature version of the speaker of "Essay on Deity" or "To Man," it is by no means a monotonous one. In the first place, the tone of voice in the poems ranges from icily logical and reflective ("The Midnight Meditation" and "The Fountain") to passionate ("The Ballad of the Scarecrow Christ") to whimsical ("Able, Baker, Charlie, Et. Al.") to satirical (both Horatian and Swiftian—"Childe Roland, Etc." and "Plot Improbable, Character Unsympathetic"). A second kind of variety results from variations in techniques of depiction ranging from direct conveyance of impressions (such as the feeling of impending doom and the chaos of World War II in "Ice Age" or of the cold brilliance of winter in "Winter Marketplace") to the creating of hallucination and phantasmagoria ("The Mirror Men" and "The Four Black Bogmen").

Finally, and most centrally, there is considerable variety in the kinds of activities the poems imitate. All of their activities are serious ones, in spite of the varieties of tone. The range includes insights and contemplations about death; World War II (as the particularization of a universally recurring experience); the quality of the age; the awakening to evil; the nature of knowledge; the meaning of the infinite; and man in relationship to the earth.[2] Twelve of the poems, taken together, are as consistent a testament of hopelessness, one which cannot be dismissed, as has been assembled anywhere: "Last Autumnal," "Ice Age," "Horror Story," "The Midnight Meditation," "The Mirror Men," "Poem," "The Night There Was Dancing in the Streets," "Plot Improbable, Character Unsympathetic," "Elegy (In Mem. Dr. P. F. S.)," "Jack in the Box," "The Pole," and "The Four Black Bogmen."

None of the remaining eleven poems offers much of a contrast in the matter of hope. "On an Adagio by Beethoven" notes that, though "Bitter is the fate of man," Beethoven's music, unable to alter it, transforms and ennobles the essential sorrow it conveys; "The Ballad of the Scarecrow Christ" ends on a hopeful note with Christ's church stripped to its bare

essentials and reborn but only at such a distance in time as
these lines tell:

> Now all the aureoled saints and martyrs
> Had breathed but one breath of eternal bliss
> And the damned who dance the dance of the burning
> Had screamed for twelve eternities
>
> And so much earthly time had passed
> As turns green forest into coal
> And that coal into diamond
> And that diamond into dust . . ." (60)

Some of the poems are primarily concerned to convey "conditions" or "objects"; and these are less concerned (a matter
of emphasis) with the concepts or insights they give rise to.
In other poems, the concepts and insights are more important;
in still others, the emphasis is about equally divided. A good
example of the first kind is "Ice Age" which depicts, in images
and metaphors, the sense of impending doom which preceded
World War II:

> Winter fell on Europe. The snow sifted,
> Gradual infiltration, incessant whispering,
>   flakes circulating innumerable as ru-
>   mors and lies,
> Masking cities, falsifying all shapes, freez-
>   ing
> Fear to a false calm, constricting
> The continent under a heavy peace like ice . . .
>
> Helpless as spectators at a cinema
> We watched history unwind from rapid spools.
> And in the cafes at dusk, the newsboys crying
> Brought the brute fear, sharp as a heart
>   attack . . . (42)

Then the war begins suddenly; the tension is lifted; and the
reader is treated to a portrait of man who has abdicated his
humanity and gone to war. There is nothing in Swift more
terrible than this portrait:

> This boy, drunken, whimpering:
> "Here am I; a prostitute and a drunkard
> Made me for lewdness' sake, like a vile
>   cartoon.
> My life has gained me these small coins
>   earned in lavatories.
> Now the bombs offer me equality; I fear it." (43)

Finally, the poem's speaker relates the sense of the war's chaos; and we have a poignant contrast between what has happened and what life was before the holocaust:

> Only the mad within their whitewashed cells,
> Made gentle by violence, or violent still
> Struggling within the grasp of giant dreams,
> These who suffer, falsely translating thought,
> Watch their world grow plausible, at last
>   confirmed.
>
> .   .   .   .
>
> How every animal knows the approach of death:
> Man also, shown the axe, the block, now
>   knows it.
> As field and woodland were but flowery ways
> The beast must travel to the bloody room,
> This way our summers and our winters led us,
> This way the child's game in the garden, and
>   the bed of love,
> The stair ascending and the stair descending,
> This way all roads ran, and all signposts
>   pointed.
> Asunder. (44-45)

The gain in depth and richness from the Eliot allusions in the last lines is evident; but we notice, too, the verse, which places its accents with great effect; produces an accompanying melody of "I" sounds; and employs a multiplicity of alliterative patterns. "Winter Nightfall" is another example which evokes an unbearable winter brightness and only secondarily, though with great power, relates its coldness with mortality. The first stanza is enough to make my point:

> January hangs glowing glass
> Icicles at eaves and sills.
> Day lifts past broken blinds and chimneys.
> But high west-spaces glitter yet
> And cast such influence beyond night
> That folk blaze in the brilliant cold,
> And beggars shuffle astral snows;
> The cur at street's end, shivering, chill,
> Burns in as pure furious light
> As stars or absolute Beings wear
> But sniffs a dazzling refuse still. (46)

To the second category, the poems in which concepts dominate, belong "The Fountain," where the concept of water as substance informs and organizes the whole poem, and, in turn, is particularized and made moving by it. The same is true with the longer and somewhat more emotional, though no less reflective, "The Midnight Meditation." The pervasive concept is that in infinite time all things recur in endless cycles (given endless change; limited matter which is conserved, and unlimited duration, all possible combinations of matter will be repeated endlessly). Such an abstraction as this is perhaps even less moving in itself than the idea behind "The Fountain." As Olson's poem gives it life, the thought is terrifying and appalling to contemplate. The poem closes:

> I thought once I should have at a man's age
> Some wisdom hard and pure as a diamond
> To make the center of a new steadfast world,
> . . . .
> And perhaps after all I have it: at last
>   recognizing
> The treadmill as a treadmill: asking of my
>   empty journeys
> Nothing, in the end, but to spare my private nobility;
>
> Dwelling at last in a house on the cloudy
>   brink
> Where the windows offer no prospect,
> And the balconies give on nothing;

> Knowing that though we speak with our old
> sophistry
> Of the dawn of hope, the dawn comes endlessly,
> Day after trailing day, but our hope never. (52)

In the last category, the poems in which emphasis seems equally divided between direct conveyance and informing concepts, are "The Mirror Men" and "The Crucifix." "The Mirror Men" is an imagistic essay in epistemology in which the speaker discovers that he cannot distinguish between self and other; all things, in a Kantian *reductio ad absurdum*, reflect only the knower in a frightening confusion. The poem is as much concerned with conveying the hallucinatory condition of its narrator, whose state certainly modifies the imagery, as it is with the epistemological difficulty which causes it. The poem in part reads:

> —Phantoms in the candleshine? the usual
> Living portraits of the haunted castle?
> —Mirrors; mirrors everywhere; in each,
> Like puppet in its cabinet, his reflection
> Selves, selves beyond number, mocked with dumbshow antic
> His agony and fright; all, all with faces
> Lugubrious and absurd as tragic masks. (54-55)

In "The Crucifix," the sight of a silver crucifix reminds the speaker of the actual crucifixion; and he recreates the scene:

> . . . think of the actual scene
> Friday, Friday the thirteenth, as some think
> Hot and bright at first, but gradually darkening and chilling;
> The rock and sway of a great packed crowd,
> A crowd like any other that comes to witness executions,
> With market-baskets and bundles and purses
> and other tokens of lives that would
> be resumed
> After this interruption; a crowd with children and dogs
> Crawling in and out through the forest of legs.
> Think of the straining, the craning to see as hammers and nails
> **Behaved after the fashion of hammers and nails,**

Though the nails went through veins and flesh and wedged
   bones apart.
And then the cross raised, the third of that day, displaying to
   all eyes
(Eyes glittering or sombre, lust-lit or
   horror-struck, but mostly curious)
The head, turning slowly from side to side,
As always with the pinned or the empaled,
The eyes already rapt with suffering,
The hands nailed like frogs to the rough cross-timber,
The feet spiked to the foot-block, amid cries and murmurs
The cross raised; and after a little while,
The eyes of the spectators straying, their
   lips beginning to discuss, other executions, and other
   things than executions,
The crowds slowly dispersing, the best parts being over,
Leaving only a few whispering at the foot of the cross
   in the gathering dusk, and the Roman soldiers,
To whom this was another execution,
Glad to relax after the anxieties of maintaining discipline.
   (80-81)

This account of the crucifixion is followed by a moving account
of the solitude of the cross and of the slowness and pain of
Christ's death. Then follows the thought, the poem's insight,
the unguessable quality of the suffering of Christ:

Think of this, gaze your fill on it, then remember
It is the Christ that sanctifies the Cross,
Not the Cross, Christ; and remember, it is not
Preeminence in pain that makes the Christ
(For the thieves as well were crucified)
No, but the Godhead; the untouchable unguessable unsuffering
Immortality beyond mortality,
Which feigns our mortality as this silver feigns it,
And of which we are ignorant as that multitude;
For the pain comes from the humanity; the pain we know;
The agony we comprehend; of the rest, know nothing. (81)

III   Plays and Poems, 1948-58 and Later Plays

Plays and Poems, 1948-58[3] contains the only collection of

Elder Olson's plays; and nineteen new lyrics, in addition to eleven reprinted from *The Scarecrow Christ,* are also in this volume. The plays were not well received though Paul Engle found them "lively, amusing, lyrical."[4] James Dickey, whose review of *Plays and Poems* is the most favorable recent review of Olson, thought the plays too full of "gimmicks"; but he liked the lyrics so well that he said this of Olson: "I keep asking myself why his work is not better known. I can think of no adequate answer, and must leave Olson's relative neglect a mystery, trusting I have done what I could to rectify what seems to me a really shameful situation and hoping to enlist the aid of Time."[5]

The plays are really, in Olson's own terms, "pseudo-dramas." The people in them do not come alive; they seem mere masks. I like best the very brief "The Shepherd and the Conqueror" which dates back to *The Cock of Heaven* where it was Part III in illustration of the Sin of Anger. It should be mentioned, however, that *The Carnival of Animals* won a joint award of the Academy of American Poets and the Columbia Broadcasting System in 1957. This play does create an air of macabre phantasy which is quite disturbing, and it is more moving than the other plays. It should also be noted that Olson's rendition of the speech of the youth of South Side Chicago is very good. The Sorcerer's Apprentices, in the play named after them, speak in this language; and the play recounts the parable of "the man of Brass" whom they set in motion in spite of warnings from the skull of Aristotle, who may very well be that last nicety of science, the hydrogen bomb.

Olson soon became aware of the thinness and abstractness of these plays, for the 1962 reworked version of *The Illusionists* was published as *A Crack in the Universe.*[6] The theme, the conflict of the rights of the individual versus the welfare of the state, is the same as that in *The Illusionists;* but the play has been enlarged and enriched, especially in characterization. The chief addition is Walter, a human scientist, now a servant to the masters of the illusion machines, who years before had discovered that "matter is a question of wavelengths; and all kinds of wave-lengths can exist in the same place, just as you can have all kinds of radio and television broadcasts in the air at once." Walter also invented a "selenium" mirror through which he passed to the wave-length of the illusionists, leaving the mirror behind, the "crack in the universe," through which the illusionists are "fishing" for men to provide "materials" to keep themselves alive. Each of those partaking of the illusion machines has had to furnish as much of his flesh as he could and stay alive, but there is now a shortage of flesh and a crisis has developed.

Another addition to the play is Rowell, a young and highly educated man, who has become aware of the illusory quality of life on earth and is repelled by it. Rowell, who might well be the speaker in Olson's lyric "The Rebellion," provides the link between the wave-length of the earth and that of the illusionists. The character of Forsell, originally a man who had come from earth deliberately to sell his people, becomes a well-meaning Babbitt with no more moral sense than his prototype, who, like his real-life counterparts, is shocked at the anarchic views of Rowell. Even the roles of the illusionists have been reenforced: Septimus, the governor; Lilia, the perfection of sexuality who is enjoyed by all the men on the illusion machines; Sporla, who "loses control" and is humanized; and Hari, her lover, are drawn with the right degree of remoteness and lifelikeness to be believable. *A Crack in the Universe* is not only first-class science fiction; it is witty, should play well; and, above all, it makes clear the direction in which man is heading: away from happiness and toward illusion. The epigraph to the play is from Aristotle's *Ethics*: "But as to what happiness is, they disagree." To Aristotle, only reasonable men are happy; and the truly reasonable man has no illusions.

The Abstract Tragedy, A Comedy of Masks,[8] is Olson's latest play, 1963; and it is his most well-developed and successful one. The play is peopled with characters from early Italian comedy and French pantomine, Pierrot, Polichinelle, Harlequin, Pantaloon, and Columbine; but in Olson's conception each of them is not only particularized with a gain in emotional potential but represents an aspect of man and his experience. Olson wants us to accept his characters as real people: "The charac-

ters are supposed to be, not the conventional characters of
the comedy of masks, nor the abstractions written about by
Verlaine, Dowson and others, but a group of actors who have
played set roles until they have identified themselves with
them. The traditional names and costumes should therefore
never be allowed to obscure the fact that these are real people,
living a hand-to-mouth existence while practising their profession obscurely in one small town after another."[9]

Indeed, the condition of the players is cause for profound
pity. The time is the eighteenth century; the setting, the stable-
loft of an inn; and the actors have not been able to work for
thirty-six days because of the rain. They are literally reduced
to starvation; and the rain, which falls throughout the play,
furnishes an accompaniment to their misery. The following excerpt is from the scene in which they have been told that the
landlord of the inn has confiscated their properties:

> PIERROT: But we can't play
> Without those things—how can we play
> Without those things? If we can't play,
> How can we pay?
>
> POLICHINELLE: That's right—how can we pay
> If we can't play?
>
> PANTALOON: How, indeed?
> I tried to get him to listen to reason;
> It's no use.
>
> PIERROT: What'll we do?
> What in the world are we going to do?
> It's a trap.
>
> PANTALOON: It *is* a trap.
>
> PIERROT: We can sit and listen to the rain.
> We can sit here in the rotten straw
> Of the stable-loft of an old inn
> And listen to the stable rats
> Rustling in the rotten straw
> And rot ourselves; until they come
> To throw us into prison-straw.
> To listen to the prison-rats
> And rot there with the rotting straw
> There'll never be another show.[10]

The play, at the level of characterization, seems a comedy; it has no tragic heroes or heroines; but its portrayal of and its message about the condition of mankind, are serious and disturbing. Each of the protagonists has a secret wish. Polichinelle's secret thoughts are wholly concerned with sexuality; specifically he longs for Columbine, who, in this play, is the wife of Pantaloon. Pantaloon's secret wish is to be heroic; but, as an exemplum of man's capacity for heroism, he is discouraging, since he has never even had the courage to touch his wife. As leader of the players, he is responsible for the debts they have incurred; and, within the play, he makes a deal with the landlord to trade his wife's body for a full wineskin and remission of the debts. Pierrot represents man's intellect, and his secret wish is to understand "reality." His inability "to stand very much reality," or to come close to understanding it in any sense, is an appalling comment on all men. Harlequin, the traditional clown, symbolizes Fate. Harlequin, as a person, thinks he is far more prepared to benefit mankind than anyone else, and his secret wish is to do so. Fate, however, proves blind in this and all other instances. Columbine and the landlord, finally, represent the hard reality against which all such idealists as the other characters must run.

Olson movingly presents all these ideas by having the rainbound characters act out a play within the play in which Harlequin offers, in his role as Fate, to grant each of the others his secret wish. Momentarily, he makes Pantaloon feel like a king; Pierrot, like a wise man; and Polichinelle, the possessor of Columbine. First of all, he makes Pantaloon ruler of himself by forcing him to make a choice. Olson is saying, with Pantaloon as illustration, that the only source of nobility for man is the ability to make meaningful choices. Furthermore, as Harlequin puts it, even to refrain from choosing is a form of choice. The choice Harlequin gives Pantaloon is between life and death. He has three black boxes in a net, and he tells Pantaloon he must choose one; but, if he chooses the empty one, he is to die. Of course, all three boxes are empty; and Pantaloon's choice, as is any choice about death, is only an illusion. When Harlequin convinces him that he must stand by his choice, Pantaloon demands to be killed:

PANTALOON: If this is mischief, to give madmen
    An eerie cause for laughter,
    I have nothing to say.
    But if you are in earnest—if
    You have indeed become my Fate—
    I will tell you, I am in earnest, too,
    I have heard of men who went to death
    As to their mistress; I could not do that,
    I dread the dark dust-bin of the grave,
    I dread to lie in darkness there
    With rags, bones, bottles, broken things;
    I dread it. Yet if to live
    Is still to inhabit a refuse heap,
    I dread that more; let the grave have me
    And shape the elements that made me
    to something better.

HARLEQUIN: Withdraw or die.

PANTALOON: I will not withdraw. I have chosen.
    In a blind choice where there was no choice
    I still have chosen. You cannot undo that.

HARLEQUIN: Well, I'll withdraw.

PANTALOON: And you cannot;
    If you owe me death, pay me; pay me.[11]

Harlequin then maneuvers Pierrot into stabbing Pantaloon with a wooden sword; when he falls, he is apparently bleeding and dying.

In the sequel, Pierrot, convinced that Pantaloon has become noble, thinks he himself has attained a view of reality; but Harlequin thinks otherwise:

HARLEQUIN: Why did you do it?
PIERROT: He was suffering.
    I couldn't stand to see him suffer.
HARLEQUIN: A clown's act—done upon a clown.
    I was only showing him his true self,
    I was only doing what God and Fate do
    To everyone of us, every day.
    Only showing him what he was.
    —A clown's act—done upon a clown!

PIERROT: No. No. If Fate's a Harlequin
    —A dirty Harlequin like you—
    And perhaps it is—we can still beat it.
    You told him he was noble
    And he believed you and was noble;
    His choice was a noble choice, his death
    A noble one; he was noble in spite of you.
HARLEQUIN: It's a lie; there's nothing noble;
    There's nothing but reality—
PIERROT: And reality can be noble.
    I learned that through your dirty trick;
    Reality can be noble.[12]

In the meantime, with Pantaloon and Pierrot occupied in discussion, Polichinelle has been sent after his heart's desire, Columbine, who has gone down from the loft. At the end of the play within the play, all is clarified: Polichinelle climbs back into the loft disillusioned and a physical wreck; Columbine and the landlord have beaten him and then copulated in his presence. Pantaloon is not dead, but drunk. The blood Pierrot let was only wine from the wineskin that the landlord had given him and that he had concealed beneath his coat and had drunk as he lay on the floor. Pierrot, with his human intellect, remains convinced, in spite of everything, that Pantaloon was heroic. Harlequin, as an impotent fate, makes the final comment, and the players continue playing their roles as before:

HARLEQUIN: Failed; failed
    Failed in everything I tried;
    Only the old comedy again:
    Everybody unhappy with the happy ending.
    (He retrieves his hat, replaces it on his head.)

    I did no better than Fate or God,
    It's really very humiliating.
    I wish that the whole universe
    And every living thing within it
    Was one cockroach—just one cockroach;
    I'd stamp on it—stamp on it—and be finished.[13]

The new lyrics in *Plays and Poems, 1948-58* are somewhat, though not markedly, more hopeful than those of *The Scarecrow Christ;* but they are the utterances of the same voice that had spoken in the earlier poems. Two exceptions are "London Company," the narrator of which is one of the settlers of the new world, and the very moving "The Cry." "The Cry" is narrated, and it presents a character other than the narrator who is named Martin whose behavior in the poem is modified by the presence of his wife. The poem is thus an instance of two people acting and interacting in a closed situation. The poem portrays a moment in the life of Martin, a moment which could only follow from a particular sequence of events and which will have permanent and serious consequences. Martin has just received a telegram from the government telling him that his son has been killed; the moment which follows, one of intense shock, is followed by revulsion at a senseless and cruel universe.

More typical of this volume in technique are a number of brief poems, each of which portrays an insight of a philosophic nature. "The Exegesis" is as imagistic essay on the conservation of matter and substance in a pre-Socratian vein; and "The Altar" is a comment on the ineffectiveness of man's attempts to placate the "gods" of the earth:

> I found the ruined altar in the glen,
> Nearly returned, now, to brute natural rock.
> A bush blazed on it, like an altar-fire.
> A shrine cast down as by an enemy;
> Its coronals and garlands broken away,
> Its columns fallen, shattered; all as if
> The only carvers had been wind and rain.
>
> A bitter token: that faith, that labor spurned.
> I stood remembering how the robed priestly waves
> Chant in strange processionals, and the wild earth
> Year after year renews mysterious rites
> To powers that make no covenant with man,
>
> Gods barbarous and implacable, that destroy
> Even what we would consecrate to them,

And only in shrines made pure of us at last
Place for themselves a proud offering of their own. (144)

"The Cocks of Babylon" argues *a fortiori* the relationship
of the conservation of matter to that of spirit: "Every particle
of the universe / Was forged to outlast eternities; / Not one
can be destroyed, not one; / Is the spirit less than these? /
Cried the cocks of Babylon" (155). Also in the category of
philosophic poems is one, somewhat less abstract, but none-
theless universal which is short enough to quote:

In Defense Of Superficiality

Respect all surfaces. The skater is
Safe until his superficiality
Fails. A bridge, the frailest,
Is better than the abyss. The green earth's pleasant,
Very pleasant, isn't it? Don't dig.
Friendship and love are surfaces. Respect them.

All surfaces are smooth seas, and the ship
Moves to music, the sea is shimmering strings,
The sun strums golden wires, and the wind sings,
All mariners must be dancers to such minstrelsy,
Until the prow too curious probes too deep
And music ends and light ends but the sea
Goes on and on and in the whirlpool's round
The dancers go on dancing without sound.

Accept this final bubble,
From one drowned.

Three longer poems are also concerned with ideas: two of
them, "The Last Entries in the Journal" and "A Nocturnal for
his Children," are quite like the thought-filled poems of the
earlier collections; but each has a fresh setting and circumstances which determine, in part, the way in which the activity of the poem is depicted. "The Last Entries in the Journal"
consists of twenty-five short lyrics, each of which contains a
separate insight into human experience or illustrates some
speculation on the nature things—thoughts as they might be
jotted down by someone keeping a journal while irrevocably

lost, alone, waiting for death. The poem's setting and its circumstances are the condition of humanity.

"A Nocturnal for his Children" is told in the earnest tone
with which a father might address his children (their presence
as listerners is a factor in the effect of the poem); and, appropriately, the poem contains brief, three-beat lines and simple
language. The third of these longer poems is "A Valentine for
Marianne Moore" which is less particularized and more directly argumentative than any of the other poems. In fact,
it is closer to a philosophic essay than to a mimetic poem; its
metaphor has the force of true analogy, and its basic argumentative device is inference bolstered by the authority of Plato
and Aristotle. The final stanza must have pleased Miss Moore:

> True beauty is most truly praised
> By the glass which is most true.
> Madam, this glass is mine,
> The loveliness within is you.
> Accept this for your valentine.
> It has my heart's shape, and no more;
> I scorn to dress it with the common lace;
> Let it have no grace but your grace. (162)

To return to "A Nocturnal for his Children" and "The Last
Entries in the Journal," the speaker in "A Nocturnal" is concerned about telling his children what his experience and
study have brought him to think about life. Humble and
truthful, he makes no attempt to soften his thought; but he
is able to hold out a hope at the end. He begins with a con-
fession.

> Night after night, alone,
> My daughters and my son,
> I ponder the starry sky,
> The Book of Heaven, with all
> Its burning charactery,
> Its scripture of suns and moons.
>
> I watch the seas unroll
> Again and again their scroll,

> I brood upon the runes
> In the mountain-folds
> And the words graven in the hills
>
> Till dazzled and full of shame
> Dull scholar that I am
> I turn away at last
> Knowing I cannot read
> One word, one character
> Of what is written there. (147)

After this grave opening, he tells of the vastness of the universe and how, for all its vastness, it may be only an atom in a still vaster one, and of how each man walks between two eternities, He then says that some find good in the design of the universe and are blest in their certainty:

> they
> Who see the great vortices
> Of turning worlds and the least
> Atoms of the least atom obey
> The perpetual command
> Of the silent voice
>
> . . . .
> They know both good and ill
> Execute one will.
>
> . . . .
> they know
> Winter as a sign
> Of Eden returning like spring. (148)

But there are also those who, perhaps not so blest,

> see
> The universe like a fire
> Raging out of control
> And all things are its fuel;
> A fire that warms nothing,
> Lights nothing, is purposeless,
> But its flames must storm and storm
> Till all is consumed, and it dies. (149)

The thought in this tremendous simile is terrifying in itself,
and its imagistic embodiment powerfully augments that terror.
Those who see the universe in these terms also argue from
"design," but do so in patterns which find "the lamb / Fash-
ioned cunningly / And the lion as cunningly / Devised to strike
it down" (150).

The father concludes by admitting that he does not know
if either of these views is true; but, though he is denied knowledge, he can distinguish between good and evil, and he cannot
imagine God as less able than himself. The poem concludes,
in a Kantian vein, with the faith of one denied knowledge;
one who believes he sees signs in the world of a spiritual
evolution:

> Not in God's image was man
> First created, but in
> Likeness of a beast;
> Until that beast became man,
> All travailled in death and pain
> And shall travail still
> Till man be the image of God
> And nothing shall transform
> Man to this image, but love;
> And this I believe is God's will.
>
> And all shall work that will:
> Planet and planet shall spin,
> Atom and atom, until
> The scriptures of heaven and earth,
> Mountain and ocean, spell
> The one unnameable Name
> Of one we know nothing of,
> Save what we learn from love,
> Love that has one name only
> Since love makes all things one
>
> As it makes us one,
> My daughters and my son. (151)

"The Last Entries in the Journal," in keeping with its prem-
ise, is not a continuous argument; however, a thread of hope,
albeit a tenuous one, spun by a mind which knows the worst,

runs through it. The tone ranges in the individual "entries"
from reasoned, to passionate, to wonder struck; and this range
gives the poem the dynamics of a structure. The optimism
of these calm and rich lines is a hard-earned one:

> Problem: to hear the battering storm as music,
> But never, drunk with harmony, be deaf
> To all the dissonances compounding harmony.
> Except as establishing the principle
> Of harmonies to be. Pain, too, is meaningless
>
> . . . .
>   Discord is meaningless
> Save as preluding peace, and suffering
> Itself ennobles no one; it degrades,
> Unless it is resolved at last to joy. (165-66)

The thought and feeling are at other moments much more
intense, as in the following three "entries" in which there is a
progression of self-reproach and a bitter resolution:

XV

> Autumn again; again and yet again.
> Am I for this, then? To count seasons out?
> I thought, once, I should name the secret names
> Of all that is, and keep all being safe,
> Locked in the little thunders of the tongue.

XVI

> For this, that history of torment? Soul's-
>   rape of birth,
> Agony and shame of growth?
> Cast up, panting, on white shores of flesh?
>   Ship-wrecked by my lusts,
> —That's my blood on the world, I have trailed
>   it everywhere,
> You may read my whole history in it. Let me
>   put on my mask;
> Ugly, perhaps; but I can't speak truth without
>   it.

XVII

> Peace, poor soul, peace, pèace, for God's sake, peace;

> This is your world, and you were made for it;
> Why should the dung-beetle quarrel with the dung? (167)

Though no sampling can do justice to the power of "The Last Entries in the Journal," the final "entry" stands alone as one of the most perfect of Olson's "imagistic lyrics of thought"; the insight it conveys is remarkable; and the imagery depicts it with a brilliance compounded of star light on snow. The preciseness with which such a grand and essentially abstract thought is presented evokes both surprise and wonder:

> Arise and look, the dream said; it is there.
> And dreaming still, he rose and went outdoors.
> All the air glistened with stars and snow.
>
> The farthest star shot down a ray and struck
> The nearest snow-flake, that itself a star,
> And at its center kindled a new star
>
> That lived just long enough to flash one ray
> Back to the farthest star. There you have it.
> Things with no connection, the immense, the minute,
> The most perduring, the most transitory
> Somehow connected, across unimaginable gulfs. (169)

III   Collected Poems, *1963*

The *Collected Poems* of 1963[14] includes selections from all of Olson's previous volumes of poems and nineteen new lyrics. The new poems are more various and more experimental than the earlier ones; and, while none is so powerful as some of the more intense pieces in *The Scarecrow Christ,* or in *Plays and Poems,* they have a freshness which is exciting. It is not so much, in many cases, that the situations are fresh but that the treatment brings them to life. In "Plaza Mexico" and "Taxco," for example, Olson has achieved better than any place else a goal he set for himself in the first poem of his first volume, "Prologue to his Book":

> To speak, to say
> With speech, This way,
> See, see, It was this way.

The two poems are successful in conveying a direct sense of aspects of Mexico,—its sights, sounds, smells, its texture, the tastes of its foods—and, as always with Olson, the insights to be gained through the senses.

"Plaza Mexico" recreates the bull fight and penetrates to its central attraction. At the beginning, the antiquity, grace, and whimsicality of the spectacle are caught:

> At half past four a trumpet stills the crowd.
> A man in the court-dress of Cervante's day
> Rides out upon a daintily stepping bay,
> Lifts his hat before the President's box,
> Bows on his curtseying horse, catches the ribboned
> Keys to the toril locks,
> Bows, withdraws.
>   Band-music erupts.
> A tiny army makes its brief parade;
> The matadors in armor of brocade,
> The tinsel pawn, the basin helmeted
> Quixotes upon quilted jades;
> Last, a jingling team of mules.

And at the end:

> The bull
> Broods in his raying spears;
> Tail up, charges; charges once again;
> Ponders, at last in doubt;
> Then, the sword-hilt plain
> Amid the barbs, the blood,
> Turns away, moves to the barriers;
> There
> Beds down; at the knife-blow, rolls
> Over, legs in air.
> The mules jingle in and jingle out
> And the crowd stirs, suddenly
> Relieved that, after all,
> It has not seen what it half hoped to see. (175)

"Taxco" details so many particulars in which essential things about Mexico are contained that it has the vitality of a live experience even in abridgment. The contrasts and strange juxtapositions which characterize Mexico are all captured:

> A rose cathedral lifts its twin bell-towers,
> Swings bells of weathered bronze, intones, intones
> Stone the color of an album-rose
> Shapes, in its fantasies, crossed papal keys,
> Dreams awhile of John baptising Christ,
> Sets spirals on pilasters to ascend
> Through cherubs, anthemia, and evangelists
> To airy belfries where grave angels gaze.
> At last both faith and science crown the whole:
> The cross stands paramount with the lightning-rod.
>
> .   .   .   .
>
> Perhaps the land
> Has its true image in some silent thing.
> The moon illumines mountains and mountainous
>   cloud,
> And all the forests stand in silent light,
> But for some cloud-like reason I recall
> A woman in prayer before a crucifix.
> The world, I reflect, is merely what it means
> Remembering the passion in that wrinkled face
> Though cross and Christ were only woven straw.

The experimentation, mentioned earlier, in *Collected Poems* is primarily one of "manner." "The Attack on the Jungle Train," for example, is a little pseudo play—as are "Chess-Game," "The Side of the Bread," and "The Argument about the Decoration of the Punch Table" in which there are differentiated characters. "The Attack" depicts the indifference and brutality of nature to men, a brutality and indifference surpassed only by that of man to man; "Chess-Game" probes the nature of hatred; "The Side of the Bread" is a satiric comment on human nature and economics; and "The Argument" satirizes a contention between husband and wife in terms at once beautiful and comic.

Among lyrics which do not employ the dramatic device are "Ice-Skaters," which has the same "life is motion" principle which Stevens treated and in the same imagistic manner; "A

Dream for a Sad Lady," which presents the continuity of grief from age to age and does so in the soft and unreal imagery of dreams; and "Directions to the Armorer," which is a wry personal self-assessment.

"Poet to Reader," the final poem, both in *Collected Poems* and to be discussed here, appropriately bridges the gap between Elder Olson, the poet, and Elder Olson, the literary theoretician. "Poet to Reader" is both argumentative and expressive of wonder at the nature and power of poetry. The poem argues the nature of artistic form:

> The statue is shaped within the sculptor's brain;
> Hence it is not the marble nor the bronze,
> Though bronze and marble manifest to sense
> What else were imperceptible. Thus, once made,
> It cannot be unmade. Form survives the formed,
> In placeless Place and timeless Time of thought.
> Although no longer manifest, it Is.
> We make the imperishable of perishing things. (194)

But, more movingly, the poet wonders at the power of poetry while insisting on its imaginative nature:

> In silence, in the silent room, you read
> These words I wrote in silence, in a silent room.
> There is no voice, and yet you hear a voice
> Which does not speak, and which you cannot hear.
> Out of a placeless Place the silent speech
> Echoes in silence in a timeless Time
> And sea is changed to plain and plain to sea,
> And one world fades, another comes to be.
> What shall I build you with these syllables
> Of voiceless voice, made out of breath unbreathed?
> My power is momentary, and endures
> Only for one moment without end,
> Yet for that moment I am Prospero,
> Our minds move to one music, and are one,
> I can do all, and build all as you will. (193)

CHAPTER *10*

Elder Olson: An Assessment

A LTHOUGH I have already stated in passing most of what should be said about Elder Olson the critic and the poet, to repeat them, in summary, is proper. The school of Chicago critics of which Elder Olson is one of the originators, and to which he still belongs and is a major contributor, is already widely recognized and influential. Only the difficulty of their thought prevents them from dominating contemporary criticism. In fact, a good case can be made that they do dominate the field of literary theory—by default, if for no other reason; certainly, it would be hard to name any serious competitors.

Elder Olson is, likewise, the finest theoretical critic writing today. Again, outside the Chicago group, the competition is exceedingly meager. The complaints against Olson, and there are a number of them, stem from two main sources: First, to understand him rightly demands more than a passing acquaintance with the history of philosophy and of criticism—acquaintances which not many are willing to make. Second, there is the failure to recognize not only that, when Olson is theorizing, he is interested in the general nature of art, as well as of poetry and its forms, as philosophic inquiries that produce as precise knowledge as their subject matters will admit, but also that such concerns and inquiries constitute a legitimate branch of philosophy with its own values. Many detractors, in the fashion of Yvor Winters, instead of listening to what Olson's theories say, complain that he is not writing practical criticism.

As a matter of fact, Olson is a practical critic of the greatest skill. He makes formal analyses of great power which clearly derive from his theories and find their justification in them.

If Olson has any fault, it is in not making clear enough that—in the transition from theory to practice, whether it be as critic or poet—"what" is imitated in a poem becomes inseparable from "how" the imitation is accomplished; the most profound "what" cannot survive an effete "how." In defense of Olson, however, it should be said that the "how" of a poem is a purely individual process of the poem's "productive cause," its maker. All that can be said theoretically about "how"—other than analyses of the powers of language and the various devices of depiction—is that the methods of presentation should be appropriate and adequate to the task in hand.

Finally, there is no question in my mind that Elder Olson will eventually find a place in the front rank of American poets of this century. I do not find it so surprising as James Dickey does that Olson is not more widely known and accepted as a poet since the qualities and circumstances that contribute to quick recognition and popularity have simply not been his. There is no question of Olson's virtuosity as a versifier and maker of images, but more important is his strength of intellect which invariably chooses serious objects for which he fashions appropriate and powerful formal structures.

Notes and References

Chapter One

1. R. S. Crane, "History versus Criticism in the University Study of Literature," *English Journal*, XXIV (1935), 645-67.

2. *Ibid.*, p. 662.

3. *Critics and Criticism, Ancient and Modern*, ed. R. S. Crane (Chicago, 1952) pp. 2-3. Hereinafter, *Critics*. This book is the major source of Elder Olson's theoretical criticism.

4. *Critics*, pp. 463-545.

5. *Aristotle's Poetics and English Literature*, ed. and with an introduction by Elder Olson (Chicago, 1965), p. xxviii.

6. The material on pluralism which follows is drawn mainly from Olson's "An Outline of Poetic Theory," *Critics*, pp. 546-66, and from his essay, "The Dialectical Foundations of Critical Pluralism," *Texas Quarterly*, IX (1966), pp. 202-30.

7. Olson defends the concept "universe of discourse" and argues the ways in which such "universes" can be differentiated from one another in the *Texas Quarterly* article cited immediately above.

8. "Dialectical Foundations of Critical Pluralism," *op. cit.*, pp. 221-22.

9. *Ibid.*

10. *Ibid.*, p. 224.

11. *Ibid.*, pp. 224-25.

12. *Ibid.*, p. 225.

13. *Ibid.*

14. *Ibid.*, p. 227.

15. *Aristotle's Poetics*, p. xxvii. Olson is certainly referring to his own Platonic exercise, "A Dialogue on Symbolism," and his work on the lacunae in Longinus, "The Argument of Longinus' *On the Sublime*," *Critics*, pp. 567-94 and 232-60, respectively.

16. *Critics*, pp. 27-44.

17. *Ibid.*, pp. 83-107.

18. *Ibid.*, pp. 108-37.

19. "Recent Literary Criticism," *Modern Philology*, XL (1943), 275-83.

20. *Critics*, pp. 45-82.

21. *Ibid.*, pp. 138-44.

22. There have likewise been several attacks on the Chicago critics which I have not space to answer in detail here. Chief among the attacks are W. K. Wimsatt's "The Chicago Critics, the Fallacy of the Neoclassic Species" from *The Verbal Icon* (Lexington, 1954); rather long passages from Murray Krieger's *The New Apologists for Poetry* (Minneapolis, 1956) (see especially pp. 148-55); Walter Sutton's *Modern American Criticism* (Englewood Cliffs, N. J., 1963), though he gives a fairly accurate account of the Chicago position; and David Daiches's *English Literature* (Englewood Cliffs, N. J., 1964).

Daiches, who knew the Chicago critics personally as early as 1937 attacks, not so much the Chicago position, as what he considers the critical consequences of it. The attacks of Wimsatt and Krieger, it seems patent, are based on their distress at the philosophic professionalism of the Chicagoans and on a defensive reading of their work.

Wimsatt, for instance, accuses the Chicagoans of "intentionalism" and "affectivism." What he overlooks is that it is far different to talk about intentions and effects in isolation from art objects than it is to insist that a work of art itself is the best indication of what an author intended or that the form of a poem determines its power to produce certain effects in those who have grasped that form. Sutton and Daiches simply do not go far enough into the matter to see the long-run possibilities and flexibilities of the Chicago views.

Finally, though certainly not exhaustively, there are J. M. Gray's "Aristotle's *Poetics* and Elder Olson," *Comparative Literature*, XV (1963) and Brother James Leo Kinneavy's *A Study of Three Contemporary Theories of the Lyric* (Washington, 1956). Olson is convinced that Gray's account is based on a misreading both of himself and Aristotle: "It is curious that these charges should be brought against a philosopher who, well aware of the fundamental reason for verbal ambiguity (c. f., *De Sophist. Elench.* i 165a 11-13), took unusual measures to make his meaning plain. (There are no measures one may take against being *misread.*)" Speaking of "misreading," such a systematic misreading as that of Brother Kinneavy is almost incredible. To answer him would require an essay. He seems so intent on displaying his Latin and Greek and on developing his own hypothesis that Olson is lost in the process.

23. Elder Olson, "Recent Literary Criticism," *op. cit.*, p. 278.

24. *Ibid.*, p. 276.

25. *Ibid.*, p. 279.

26. *The Language of Poetry*, ed. by Allan Tate (New York, 1960), p. viii.

27. *Critics*, p. 140.

28. *Ibid.*, p. 48.

29. William Empson, *Seven Types of Ambiguity* (Norfolk, Conn., 1953), pp. 49-50.

30. *Critics*, p. 49.

31. *Ibid.*, p. 51.

32. *Ibid.*, p. 61.

33. *Ibid.*, p. 62.

34. *Ibid.*

Chapter Two

1. See "The Argument of Longinus' *On the Sublime*." In addition to supplying the missing portions of Longinus's argument, Olson shows his understanding of the doctrine of sublimity—that greatness of mind and language inform many kinds of works, poetic and otherwise.

2. Olson's comments on Plato's view of the poet (see esp. *Critics*, pp. 593-94) have never seemed to me quite consistent. He seems torn between his esteem for the poets and for Plato whose opinion of poetry is low. Plato's hierarchy of values is determined by his theory of knowledge which places ultimate good, beauty, and truth on an intellectual level accessible only through dialectic and beyond the reach of language.

He places man's capacity to understand perfections—such as true circularity, absolute identity, and such abstractions as infinity—immediately below the highest level and related to it in an imitatory fashion. Just below this level is the world apprehended by the senses with its natural objects and man and his works. This level, too, is related to the highest as an imitation, but one twice removed from it.

At the lowest level, though still as parts of the sense world, are imitative poems, like shadows and reflections, three times removed from the real. As all things in Plato's system are valued by their proximity to knowledge, or as they are conducive to it, the imitative poet's rank is low. Plato does admit, however, that a true poet could imitate the eternal excellences. In order to do so, however, he would have to have knowledge in a Platonic sense. As only philosophers have this sort of knowledge, he would have to be a philosopher. In Plato's view such a "poet" would be the only type with true importance though he also admitted that didactic poetry had some value. It is this view of the poet as philosopher which Olson takes in his Platonic exercise "A Dialogue on Symbolism." After he has discussed symbolism in relation to mimetic and didactic poetry, Olson's Socrates speaks of "myth-makers":

"My friend, we saw that the poet, whether mimetic or didactic, required knowledge of some sort, both of his craft and that which he represented?

Yes.

Apart from that knowledge, he could never achieve plausibility of action or character or argument?

He could not.

So long as he represents this knowledge in terms of its manifestations in particular causes, we may call him 'poet' and nothing more; a very honorable thing. But what if he seeks to convey this knowledge itself, wholly divorced from all particulars and accidents. He must needs do this by some myth or fable, and we may call him a 'myth-maker' whether he uses symbol or parable or allegory; and that is to call him both 'poet' and 'philosopher.' Surely your Yeats did this in his work *A Vision;* and Eliot, also, in his myth of Wheel and still point." (*Critics*, p. 593.)

3. "The Poetic Method of Aristotle" (*Aristotle's Poetics*, pp. 175-91.) The remarks on Aristotle's thought which follow are derived in large part from this essay, and other scattered remarks of Olson's, but I have supplemented them, in ways hopefully consistent with Olson's intepretations, from my own study of Aristotle.

4. *Aristotle's Poetics*, pp. 178-79.

5. *Ibid.*, 180-81.

6. *Ibid.*

7. *Ibid.*, p. 187.

8. See R. P. McKeon's "The Concept of Imitation in Antiquity" (*Critics*, pp. 147-75). McKeon's article is as full a treatment of this intriguing and puzzling concept as is available. *See also Aristotle's Poetics,* pp. xii-xiii n.

9. *Critics*, p. 571.

10. See Elder Olson, *Tragedy and the Theory of Drama* (Detroit,

1961) p. 150 ff.; *Critics*, p. 566, and "A Dialogue on the Function of Art in Society," *Chicago Review*, XVI (1964).

11. The criteria of value are concerned with unity, beauty, consistency, and many like factors. A point of difference with Plato can be made in the manner in which the problem of beauty is treated by the two men. A poem can only be beautiful in Plato's view insofar as it is based on *knowledge* of the beautiful. For Aristotle, who is considering what Plato might call the phenomenological aspects of things, "beauty is a matter of size and order."

12. *Aristotlle's Poetics*, p. 186.

13. *Ibid.*, pp. 186-87.

14. *Ibid.*, p. 188.

Chapter Three

1. Elder Olson, "Hamlet and the Hermeneutics of Drama," *Modern Philology*, LXI (Feb., 1964), 225-26.

2. *Critics*, p. 63.

3. *Ibid.*, p. 65.

4. *Ibid.*, p. 66.

5. Depending on their concern with knowledge or action, the arguments of didactic poems can be seen to be either dialectical, practical, or rhetorical.

6. *Ibid.*, p. 554.

7. *Ibid.*

8. *Ibid.*, p. 555.

9. Elder Olson, *The Theory of Comedy* (Indiana, 1968).

10. *Critics*, p. 556.

11. *Tragedy and the Theory of Drama*, p. 154.

12. *Ibid.*, p. 156.

13. *Ibid.*, p. 560.

14. *American Lyric Poems*, edited and with an introduction by Elder Olson (New York, 1964), pp. 1-2.

15. *Ibid.*, p. 4.

16. *Ibid.*, pp. 3-4.

17. *Ibid.*, p. 4.

18. *Critics*, p. 79.

19. Elder Olson, "Louise Bogan and Leonie Adams," *Chicago Review*, VIII (1954), **p. 77 n.**

20. *Ibid.*

21. *Ibid.*, p. 79 n.

22. *Critics*, p. 80. Hume maintains there are only perceptions

(impressions) and ideas which are copies of them and necessarily less vivid. Olson thinks (see *Critics*, p. 584) that Hume confuses "idea" with the Aristotelian "phantasm which accompanies thought." However, that mental images are less vivid, regardless of how they are considered, is what is at issue here.

23. *Critics*, p. 81.

24. *Ibid.*

25. *Ibid.*

26. *Ibid.*

27. *Ibid.*, p. 586.

28. *Ibid.*, p. 591.

29. *Ibid.*, p. 68.

30. *Ibid.*, p. 71-42.

31. See, "Hamlet and the Hermeneutics of Drama," for a detailed account of the ways in which interpretation is determined by this distinction. An excellent practical example is Norman Maclean, "Episode, Scene, Speech, and Word: The Madness of Lear," *Critics*, pp. 595-616.

32. *Critics*, p. 73.

33. *Ibid.*, p. 76.

34. *Ibid.*

35. .*Ibid.*, pp. 563-64.

36. I am thinking especially of Murray Krieger's contentions in *The New Apologists for Poetry*, p. 96 n.

37. *Critics*, pp. 565-66.

38. "A Dialogue on the Function of Art in Society," p. 66.

39. Elder Olson has said substantially the same thing in an essay on Wallace Stevens, *College English*, XVI (1955), 395-402, and in *Tragedy and the Theory of Drama*, pp. 149-50.

40. "A Dialogue on the Function of Art in Society," p. 67.

41. *Ibid.*

42. *Ibid.*

43. *Ibid.*, p. 69.

44. *Ibid.*, p. 70.

45. *Ibid.*

46. *Ibid.*

47. *Ibid*

Chapter Four

1. All parenthetical references in this chapter are to *Tragedy and the Theory of Drama, op. cit.*

2. For a fine example in which Olson emphasizes the importance of the dramatic context, too long to paraphrase here, see his analysis of Macbeth's "She should have died hereafter" speech. (*Tragedy and the Theory of Drama*, pp. 114-25.)

Chapter Five

1. All parenthetical references in this chapter are to this work.

2. An excellent comment on this matter is contained in Elder Olson, "Rhetoric and the Appreciation of Pope," *Modern Philology*, XXXVII (1939), p. 34 n. I will quote in part:

"Although the term 'translation' is usually defined as the rendering of a literary structure in different diction, certain loosenesses of its application have extended its meaning to include both imitation and adaptation. In its broadest sense, translation is the construction of a literary work similar in some respect to a given work or a given kind of work; hence there are as many modes of translation as we distinguish qualitative parts of the work to be translated, or, to put it differently, as there are respects in which we take works to be similar. Thus if we distinguish plot, character, diction, and thought as qualitative parts of the epic, the equivalences between original and translation may be stated in terms of these; the criteria of translation *qua* translation would be derived, in any case, from the fact that a translation is dependent for its character upon those aspects which the translator held either to be chiefly characteristic of a work, an author, a *genre*, or a mode of composition, or, on the other hand, to be relevant to some circumstance affecting the translator."

3. A. R. Ammons in *Poetry, A Magazine of Verse*, CII (1963), pp. 198-201.

Chapter Six

1. My discussion takes into consideration all of Olson's essays in practical criticism except the one on Louise Bogan and Leonie Adams. Limitations on length would not permit the use of this important essay.

2. Elder Olson, "Rhetoric and the Appreciation of Pope," *op. cit., pp.* 13-35. All parenthetical references in the treatment of Pope are to this essay.

3. Among them are two famous critics who had written what were, in 1939, new books about Pope: Geoffrey Tillotson, *On the*

Poetry of Pope (Oxford, 1939), and Robert Kilburn Root, *The Poetical Career of Alexander Pope* (Princeton, 1939).

4. All parenthetical references in the treatment of Yeats are to this essay which was published in the *University Review*, VIII (1942), 209-19.

5. *Tragedy and the Theory of Drama*, p. 76.

6. Elder Olson, "The Poetry of Wallace Stevens," *College English*, XVI (1955), 395-402. All parenthetical references in the treatment of Stevens are to this essay.

7. Elder Olson, "The Poetry of Marianne Moore," *Chicago Review*, XI (1957), 100-104. All parenthetical references in the treatment of Miss Moore are to this essay.

Chapter Seven

1. *The Poetry of Dylan Thomas* (Chicago, 1954). All parenthetical references in this chapter are to this work.

2. Vol. VIII, 165.

3. Vol. LX, 151.

4. Vol. XXX, 475.

5. Vol. XXXVII, 30.

6. The book was also reviewed by Paul Engle in the *Chicago Tribune* (May 2, 1954); in *Nation*, CLXéVIII (1954), 360; by G. S. Fraser, *New Statesman*, XLVIII (1954), 330; by Charles Tomlinson, *The Spectator*, (August 20, 1954), 235; in *Western Humanities Review*, VIII (1954), 165; *Canadian Literature*, XXXIV (1954), 140; *Bulletin of Bibliography*, XXI (1954), 103; *Catholic World*, CLXXX (1954), 159; *Essays in Criticism*, V (1954), 164-68; *Times Literary Supplement* (January 7, 1955), 10; *Papers of the Biblographic Society of America*, XLIX (1954), 90-93; *Personalist*, XXXVI (1954), 213-14; *Poetry, A Magazine of Verse*, LXXXVII (1955), 118-19. Among these, G. S. Fraser's longish review, though he finds some faults with Olson, is generally the best. He thinks ". . . what Mr. Olson does for Thomas's grand structures, particularly the sonnets, makes us forgive him for what he fails to do in detail." The worst review is the very brief one of Charles Tomlinson who gives no evidence that he has read the book.

7. Ralph Maud, *Entrances to Dylan Thomas' Poetry* (Pittsburgh, 1963), pp. 315-22.

8. Monroe C. Beardsley and Sam Hynes, "Misunderstanding Poetry: Notes on Some Readings of Dylan Thomas," *College English*, XXI (1960), 315-22.

9. H. H. Kleinman, *The Religious Sonnets of Dylan Thomas* (Berkeley and Los Angeles, 1963).

Chapter Eight

1. Yvor Winters, *The Function of Criticism* (Denver, 1957), p. 22.

2. *Poetry, A Magazine of Verse*, XXXII (May, 1928), 22.

3. *Ibid.*, xxxvi (June, 1930), p. 182.

4. *New Republic*, CIII (October 14, 1940), 534.

5. *Yale Review*, XLIV (Summer, 1955), 602.

6. Elder Olson, *Collected Poems* (Chicago, 1963), p. vii.

7. *Ibid.*, p. 178.

8. James Dickey, "The Human Power," *Sewanee Review*, LXVII (1959), 511.

9. Elder Olson, *American Lyric Poems*, p. 6.

10. Elder Olson, *A Thing of Sorrow* (New York, 1934). All parenthetical references in this section are to this work.

11. *Saturday Review of Literature*, XI (October 27, 1934), 247.

12. See, *The Poetry of Dylan Thomas*, pp. 31-33.

13. The "idealism" in this poem borders on "solipsism." The first part of it is based on the description of man in Plato's *Protagoras*, 321. Certainly Protagoras' contention that "man is the measure of all things" is involved in its epistemology.

14. There is something here, too, of the theme of the cyclic quality of nature which, connected with the idea of infinity, is displayed with overwhelming power in "The Midnight Meditation."

15. *Collected Poems*, p. 156.

16. Elder Olson, *The Cock of Heaven* (New York, 1940). All parenthetical references in this section are to this work.

17. *Poetry, A Magazine of Verse*, LVII (1940), 214.

18. *Yale Review*, XXX (Winter, 1941), 382.

19. *Collected Poems*, p. vii.

Chapter Nine

1. Elder Olson, *The Scarecrow Christ*, (New York, 1954). All parenthetical references in this section are to this book.

2. Among excellent poems which space will not permit me to treat are two on death, "Last Autumnal," and "Elegy (In Mem. Dr. P. F. S.)"; one on World War II, "The Night There Was Dancing in the Streets"; one on the age, "Horror Story"; that marvelous depiction of the awakening to evil, "The Pole"; and "Poem" which

illustrates that, while man with his "harsh history" passes, the earth remains.

3. Elder Olson, *Plays and Poems, 1948-58* (Chicago, 1958). All parenthetical references in this section are to this work.

4. *Chicago Sunday Tribune,* (January 4, 1959), p. 3.

5. "The Human Power," *op. cit.,* p. 511.

6. Elder Olson, *A Crack in the Universe, First Stage,* I (Spring, 1962), 9-33.

7. *Ibid.,* p. 26.

8. Elder Olson, *The Abstract Tragedy, A Comedy of Masks, First Stage,* II (Summer, 1963), 166-86.

9. *Ibid.,* p. 167.

10. *Ibid.,* p. 172.

11. *Ibid.,* p. 183.

12. *Ibid.,* p. 184.

13. *Ibid.,* p. 186.

14. All parenthetical references in this section are to this work. The reviews of *Collected Poems* add little to earlier ones. With the exception of that in the *London Times Literary Supplement,* (May 7, 1964), p. 396, they tend to be favorable though essentially unperceptive. The review of M. E. Rosenthal in the *New York Times Book Review,* (March 8, 1964) p. 4, comes as close as any to recognizing the consistency with which Elder Olson has been producing great poems over the past forty years or more.

Selected Bibliography

PRIMARY SOURCES

I. BOOKS

A Thing of Sorrow. New York: The Macmillan Co., 1934.
General Prosody. Chicago: University of Chicago Libraries, 1938.
  (Doctoral Dissertation)
The Cock of Heaven. New York: The Macmillan Co., 1940.
Critics and Criticism. Chicago: University of Chicago Press, 1952.
The Scarecrow Christ. New York: The Noonday Press, 1954.
The Poetry of Dylan Thomas. Chicago: University of Chicago
  Press, 1954.
Plays and Poems, 1948-58. Chicago: University of Chicago Press,
  1958.
Tragedy and the Theory of Drama. Detroit: Wayne State University
  Press, 1961.
Collected Poems. Chicago: University of Chicago Press, 1963.
American Lyric Poems. New York: Appleton-Century-Crofts, 1964.
Aristotle's Poetics and English Literature. Chicago: University of
  Chicago Press, 1965.
The Theory of Comedy. Bloomington: University of Indiana Press,
  1968.

II. ARTICLES

"Rhetoric and the Appreciation of Pope," *Modern Philology,* XXXVII
  (1939), 13-35.

"Sailing to Byzantium: Prologomena to a Poetics of the Lyric,"
  University Review, VIII (1942), 209-19.

"The Argument of Longinus' *On the Sublime,*" *Modern Philology,*
  XXXIX (1942), 225-58.

"Recent Literary Criticism," *Modern Philology,* XL (1943), 275-83.

"A Symbolic Reading of the 'Ancient Mariner,'" *Modern Philology*, XLV (1948), 275-83.

"Is Theory Possible?" *Poetry, A Magazine of Verse*, LXXI (1948), 257-59.

"The Poetic Method of Aristotle: Its Powers and Limitations," *English Institute Essays*, 1951, (1952), 70-94.

"Criticism," *Encyclopaedia Britannica*, (Copyright, 1952. Printed in all editions to date.)

"Verse," *Encyclopaedia Britannica*, (Copyright, 1952. Printed in all editions to date.)

"Education and the Humanities," *Pedagogia*, I (1953), 85-95.

"The Poetry of Dylan Thomas," *Poetry, A Magazine of Verse*, LXXXIII (1954), 213-20.

"Louise Bogan and Léonie Adams," *Chicago Review*, VIII (1954), 70-87.

"The Poetry of Wallace Stevens," *College English*, XVI (1955), 395-402, and *English Journal*, XLIV (1955), 191-98.

"The Poetry of Marianne Moore," *Chicago Review*, XI (1957), 100-104.

"Hamlet and the Hermeneutics of Drama," *Modern Philology*, LXI (1964), 225-37.

"A Dialogue on the Function of Art in Society," *Chicago Review*, XVI (1964), 57-72.

"The Dialectical Foundations of Critical Pluralism," *Texas Quarterly*, IX (1966), 202-30.

III. PLAYS

A Crack in the Universe, First Stage, I (1962), 9-33.
The Abstract Tragedy, A Comedy of Masks, First Stage, II (1963), 166-86.

SECONDARY SOURCES

(Only major works are listed here. A number of more minor works are listed in the Notes and References.)

DAICHES, DAVID. *English Literature*. Englewood Cliffs, N. J.: Prentice-Hall, Inc., 1964. Good for a sympathetic account of the Chicago Critics which, unfortunately, is not detailed enough.

KRIEGER, MURRAY. *The New Apologists for Poetry*. Minneapolis: The University of Minnesota Press, 1956. Krieger attempts, with some success, to place Elder Olson and Chicago criticism in the perspective of the modern critical scene.

SUTTON, WALTER. *Modern American Criticism*. Englewood Cliffs, N. J.: Prentice-Hall, Inc., 1963. A basically accurate account of the Chicago position.

WIMSATT, W. K. JR. *The Verbal Icon*. Lexington: University of Kentucky Press, 1954. Wimsatt is the most consistent opponent of Chicago criticism.

Index